T0312292

Cambridge Elements ≡

Elements in Sign Languages
edited by
Erin Wilkinson
University of New Mexico
David Quinto-Pozos
University of Texas at Austin

A FAMILY-CENTERED SIGNED LANGUAGE CURRICULUM TO SUPPORT DEAF CHILDREN'S LANGUAGE ACQUISITION

Razi M. Zarchy
Rocky Mountain University of Health Professions and California State University, Sacramento

Leah C. Geer
California State University, Sacramento

CAMBRIDGE
UNIVERSITY PRESS

CAMBRIDGE
UNIVERSITY PRESS

Shaftesbury Road, Cambridge CB2 8EA, United Kingdom

One Liberty Plaza, 20th Floor, New York, NY 10006, USA

477 Williamstown Road, Port Melbourne, VIC 3207, Australia

314–321, 3rd Floor, Plot 3, Splendor Forum, Jasola District Centre, New Delhi – 110025, India

103 Penang Road, #05–06/07, Visioncrest Commercial, Singapore 238467

Cambridge University Press is part of Cambridge University Press & Assessment, a department of the University of Cambridge.

We share the University's mission to contribute to society through the pursuit of education, learning and research at the highest international levels of excellence.

www.cambridge.org
Information on this title: www.cambridge.org/9781009380768

DOI: 10.1017/9781009380720

First published 2023

A catalogue record for this publication is available from the British Library

ISBN 978-1-009-38076-8 Paperback
ISSN 2752-9401 (online)
ISSN 2752-9398 (print)

A Family-Centered Signed Language Curriculum to Support Deaf Children's Language Acquisition

Elements in Sign Languages

DOI: 10.1017/9781009380720
First published online: August 2023

Razi M. Zarchy
Rocky Mountain University of Health Professions and California State University, Sacramento

Leah C. Geer
California State University, Sacramento

Author for correspondence: Razi M. Zarchy, razi.zarchy@gmail.com

Abstract: Deaf children experience language deprivation at alarmingly high rates. One contributing factor is that most are born to non-signing hearing parents who face insurmountable barriers to learning a signed language. This Element presents a case for developing signed language curricula for hearing families with deaf children that are family centered and focus on child-directed language. Core vocabulary, functional sentences, and facilitative language techniques centered around common daily routines allow families to apply what they learn immediately. Additionally, Deaf Community Cultural Wealth (DCCW) lessons build families' capacity to navigate the new terrain of raising a deaf child. If early intervention programs serving the families of young deaf children incorporate this type of curriculum into their service delivery, survey data suggest that it is both effective and approachable for this target population, so the rates of language deprivation may decline.

This Element also has a video abstract: www.cambridge.org/zarchy-geer

Keywords: sign language curriculum, early intervention, deaf education, family-centered curriculum, first and second language acquisition

ISBNs: 9781009380768 (PB), 9781009380720 (OC)
ISSNs: 2752-9401 (online), 2752-9398 (print)

Contents

1 Introduction

There is increasing scholarly work on the linguistics of signed languages. Some of this work is theoretical; through the study of signed languages, we can learn more about language generally, test linguistic theories, and even understand more about how language works in the brain depending on, or irrespective of, language modality. Other linguistic work is translated into practical, everyday uses like teaching signed languages, developing assessments, and understanding how to treat language disorders. However, the linguistic study of the needs of deaf children and their hearing families requires a more action-based approach.[1] Rather than merely documenting what happens in the language acquisition process of these children and their families, linguists can have the greatest impact on children's language outcomes by creating curricula specifically designed to teach families with deaf children. Because these families are typically in the beginning stages of learning signed languages while their children are young, teaching them evidence-based facilitative language techniques may partially make up for their beginner-level skills by enabling them to use their limited language skills strategically to provide a language-rich environment for their child. The need for accessible, language-rich environments for deaf children is especially urgent because of the language issue that is most salient within deaf communities: language deprivation (Glickman et al., 2020).

Language deprivation can result when a child is not exposed to a sufficiently accessible language from birth. Possibly the most well-known case of language deprivation is the case of the feral child "Genie" (Curtiss et al., 1974). Genie experienced severe neglect and abuse, and while she had typical hearing, her isolation prevented her from being exposed to language. As a result, she did not acquire a native language in a typical way, and this had significant impacts on her cognitive and psychosocial development. While this was an extreme case that received much attention from both the media and the research community, cases of language deprivation among deaf children are the norm rather than the exception (Hall, 2017). This has been the topic of much recent attention in the literature (Cheng et al., 2019; Glickman & Hall, 2018; W. C. Hall et al., 2017; Skotara et al., 2012, among others).

---

[1] While the prescription of "D" and "d" *deaf* used to be more clear-cut – the former describing a cultural affiliation and the latter a medical diagnosis – newer work has shown that representing this word in text is anything but (Pudans-Smith et al., 2019). Throughout this Element, unless referring to a title (e.g., Deaf Mentor) or quoting directly or indirectly a text which uses "Deaf," we have opted for the lower-case spelling, following Gale and colleagues (2021) and Lillo-Martin and Henner (2021), to be more inclusive of all individuals, regardless of hearing levels, language use, and additional disabilities.

One way to prevent language deprivation is to ensure that hearing families with deaf children have: 1) appropriate education on language acquisition in deaf children and the importance of language that is both available, meaning "in the environment," and accessible, meaning "can be processed by a sensory system" (Gárate & Lenihan, 2016); and 2) sufficient access to learn a signed language with and for their children. This Element addresses the latter. While signed language learning materials are becoming increasingly available, especially through the Internet, most of these are not focused on the specific population of hearing families with deaf children. Thus, family-centered signed language curricula are the topic of this Element. The remainder of the introduction describes deaf children and language, language learning in adults, existing resources for deaf early intervention, existing resources for learning signed languages, and suggestions for combining forces across disciplines to create a family-centered curriculum.

Before beginning, we would like to share a bit about our positionality and the lived experiences we bring to this Element. The first author is an American Sign Language (ASL)–fluent, hearing, speech-language pathologist (SLP) who has been practicing for over eleven years. He has worked predominantly within a deaf education program in a public school district for the past seven years. His primary focus has been early intervention within this deaf education program, but he has also worked with secondary-aged deaf youth and hearing children in public preschool programs. Before getting his master's degree to become an SLP, he received his bachelor's degree in linguistic anthropology, where he also studied various other languages including French, Spanish, Yiddish, and Hebrew. After wanting to learn ASL for most of his life, he was finally able to do so in graduate school and has been immersed in the local deaf community ever since.

The second author is deaf, but not from birth. It is most likely that she was hard of hearing growing up, but this was not confirmed audiometrically until later on when her hearing levels began to decline. She acquired English natively and Spanish as a heritage speaker (her maternal grandparents were native speakers). She learned ASL from a young age from deaf friends and from hearing friends with deaf parents. Her signing was more English-based early in her life, but when she got to college, she began socializing with more ASL-dominant individuals, resulting in a change in her signing style. To further her skills, she attended an ASL immersion program at the New Mexico School for the Deaf for two summers before graduating college and getting her master's degree in linguistics at Gallaudet University. She later completed a Ph.D., also in linguistics. She has worked as a university professor for six and a half years, teaching courses in ASL, ASL linguistics, deaf culture, and other deaf studies subjects. She is now predominantly an ASL user.

1.1 Deaf Children and Language

Around 90 percent of deaf children are born to hearing families (Mitchell & Karchmer, 2004), most of whom do not sign (Office of Research Support and International Affairs, 2014). Many studies have documented poor language outcomes in this population (e.g., Nittrouer et al., 2019). One of the best predictors of strong language outcomes for deaf children is high-quality early intervention services, including high-quality language instruction for their families (Sass-Lehrer et al., 2016). However, without a curriculum that serves this specific purpose, families may struggle to acquire a signed language and provide an accessible language-rich environment at home, which can have severe, lifelong consequences for their children's language outcomes (Hall, 2017; Humphries et al., 2016). Thus, families who want to learn a signed language for and with their young deaf child require a specialized instructional approach.

1.1.1 The Input Matters

Children need rich language input to acquire their first language effectively (Goldin-Meadow, 1982; Newport, 1991). Children with typical hearing and no additional disabilities acquire language effectively and effortlessly regardless of their families' communication styles. However, Nittrouer and colleagues (2019) found that deaf children acquiring oral language benefited when their parents asked more questions and were more responsive to their children's communication attempts. The researchers found that parental input had the strongest effect on children with cochlear implants, compared with hearing children and deaf children with hearing aids. It stands to reason that deaf children acquiring signed language also benefit from communication styles that provide a language-rich home environment.

It is important to assess deaf children's language input effectively because it informs the interpretation of assessment results. The results of a language input assessment can reveal how much of a child's language input has come from a given language or modality, which then informs how much of their cumulative input has been accessible and how much of their life has taken place in a state of impoverished, inaccessible language input. Assessors such as early interventionists or school-based service providers must know about a child's language input experience because it helps them to differentiate a delay resulting from a lack of input from an innate language disorder (Hall, 2020). Research shows that children's language may grow best when input from parents is at a level of linguistic complexity slightly higher than what the child currently expresses (Boyce et al., 2013), so professionals assessing deaf children's language input may consider structural aspects of that input such as the amount, rate, syntactic complexity, and semantic complexity. This information can inform recommendations they make to parents and the educational team when setting goals and choosing intervention strategies.

1.1.2 Typical Language Development in Deaf Children

Deaf children from deaf families who are fluent in signed language tend to have full, direct access to language from birth. The results of this early linguistic access are apparent in their tendency, in the absence of additional disabilities, to acquire language at the same rate as their hearing peers (Goodwin et al., 2019; Lillo-Martin et al., 2021; Lillo-Martin & Henner, 2021; Meier, 2016). For example, children exposed to signed language from birth, regardless of hearing status, typically exhibit manual babbling that becomes more complex over time and emerges into true words. Signing children and speaking children achieve two-word utterances by approximately the same ages: 18–24 months for English-speaking hearing children, for example (Brown, 2013), and 17–21 months for deaf native ASL-signing children (Lillo-Martin et al., 2017). From that point, children who have had access to language from birth develop the typical syntax for their respective languages at similar rates, regardless of language or modality. Additionally, research on children from deaf families – specifically, hearing children of deaf adults (CODAs) and deaf children with cochlear implants – shows that children raised in a signing environment who also have auditory access can become competent bimodal bilinguals: individuals who are bilingual across two different modalities (Davidson et al., 2014; Hassanzadeh, 2012; Mitchiner et al., 2012).

1.1.3 Disrupted Language Development in Deaf Children

Language deprivation syndrome is a neurodevelopmental disorder common in deaf individuals who do not get early access to their first language (W. C. Hall et al., 2017). There is evidence that language deprivation causes lifelong changes in brain structures (Cheng et al., 2018; Pénicaud et al., 2013), particularly in the pathways that link together the various regions of the brain governing language processing and syntactic structures (Cheng et al., 2019). Language deprivation also causes lifelong deficits in cognition, behavior, social-emotional development, and attention. Professionals across the health and education fields have described the concurrent phenomena of language dysfluency and apparent deficiencies in behavior and social-emotional skills in deaf individuals since the 1960s, but it has become an especially prominent part of the deaf education and psychology literature since the turn of the twenty-first century (Glickman et al., 2020; W. C. Hall et al., 2017). In 2017, W. C. Hall and colleagues proposed the term "language deprivation syndrome" (LDS) to describe individuals who present with the aforementioned constellation of severe symptoms.

Language deprivation, whether at severe enough clinical levels to be labeled as LDS (which does not yet have diagnostic criteria at the time of this writing; see Glickman et al., 2020) or not, leads to poor outcomes across areas of development, especially in language development. Deaf children who do not have full access to language from birth tend to lag behind their hearing peers in syntax, verbal reasoning, vocabulary, and reading comprehension (Santos & Cordes, 2022). Henner and colleagues (2016) found that among American children who attended schools for the deaf, children who received earlier access to language and entered schools for the deaf at younger ages were found to have superior syntax and analogical reasoning skills compared to children whose first exposure to ASL occurred later in life or who entered the schools at an older age.

Language skills are necessary to develop a wide variety of academic abilities, so poor language outcomes also lead to poor academic outcomes. For example, deaf children not exposed to a natural signed language from birth demonstrate lower math abilities than those exposed to accessible (visual) language from birth. This is likely because of the increasing linguistic demands of mathematical tasks as children age (Santos & Cordes, 2022). This link between math and language is evident in studies showing that knowledge and use of grammatical markers such as plurals may support understanding of mathematical concepts and that expressive and receptive vocabulary are linked to number word knowledge (Negen & Sarnecka, 2012, as cited in Santos & Cordes, 2022).

There is also evidence that a lack of early access to language affects cognitive development. Executive functioning is a high-level cognitive process that regulates cognition, behavior, attention, planning, problem-solving, and inhibitory control. Educators and clinicians have long noted concern for deaf children's executive functioning skills and often attributed the observed deficits to hearing loss (see M. L. Hall et al., 2017 for a brief history of this connection). However, recent investigations of executive functioning in deaf children have discovered that their executive functioning skills and related social interaction skills are actually more dependent on language access than on auditory access (Goodwin et al., 2022; M. L. Hall et al., 2017, 2018). Thus, a deaf child's language background is an important factor when considering any deficits in executive functioning, which can also cause significant disruptions to social interaction skills (Morgan et al., 2021).

1.1.4 Language Learning in Adults

The previous section described the situation of disrupted first language acquisition in deaf children from hearing families. Language outcomes in these children can be ameliorated when their families begin learning a signed language as quickly as possible (Caselli et al., 2021), but this is easier said than done. This section addresses several theories of adult second language (L2) acquisition and how they relate to the unique curriculum design best suited for this population.

The input processing (IP) theory posits that acquisition is a byproduct of comprehension (VanPatten, 2015). Thus, learners must make appropriate form–meaning connections, or correctly identify a word's meaning, as they attempt to comprehend their new language. The challenge is that learners do not always make correct form–meaning pairings, which means that language instruction needs to be designed to facilitate correct pairings. The central claim of IP is that learners arrive at the task of language learning knowing that languages have words and they attempt to search for lexical items, specifically content words, as they receive input.

The premise of IP suggests a pedagogical approach in which learners learn words, and then immediately practice comprehending them in sentences. This enables them to learn what key lexical items look like in isolation and then search for them in a stream of input immediately thereafter. This parsing is key to IP because learners must segment the input stream correctly, identify word boundaries, and correctly pair each parsed item with the correct meaning. The theory of IP also offers some explanation as to why dictionary-only learning is unlikely to be successful (Chen Pichler, 2021). In a study by Decker and Vallotton (2016), many parents of deaf children only had access to vocabulary and dictionary-like resources for learning ASL but wanted to learn word order and other aspects of the complete language. However, dictionary-only learning does not allow learners to seek out word meanings in a stream of language input, so it leaves a significant gap in learners' language-learning process.

Another theory, the declarative/procedural model (DP model), is grounded in neurobiology (Ullman, 2015). Specifically, this theory is based on the brain's memory systems, how they support language learning, and the types of learning each system underlies. Declarative memory is related to learning new information and consolidating it during sleep. This type of memory is required for learning new idiosyncratic information and explicit knowledge, and then linking information together. Declarative knowledge can be learned quickly, sometimes with a single exposure. Further exposures then strengthen knowledge and memories. Declarative memory improves during childhood, plateaus in the teen years, and then declines after early adulthood (which could partially explain why language learning is harder in adulthood). Procedural memory underlies more implicit learning for learning and consolidating new motor and cognitive skills. It is used to process activities like sequences and rules. Unlike declarative memory, procedural memory requires extended practice. With extended practice, skills become more automated and routinized.

What this suggests, and what Ullman's (2015) analysis supports, is that declarative memory is likely primary for learning vocabulary, which is why some words are retained with a single exposure. Procedural memory governs activities such as using vocabulary in sentences and producing sentences, such that the motor patterns become more fluid and automated over time. Both types of memory are necessary for a learner to produce language at a conversational level.

The final theory of L2 acquisition discussed here is related to input, interaction, and output. This work draws from scholarship on psychology related to noticing, working memory, and attention. *Input* is simply the language the learner is exposed to in communicative contexts. Learners use this input to generate linguistic hypotheses about the language they are learning. Gass and Mackey (2015) found that modifying this input, such as making it more simplistic, can aid comprehension for new learners. *Interaction* is defined as the conversations in which learners partake. It is through interaction that learners receive feedback as to the (in)correctness of their productions. *Output* is what learners produce in their new language. Foundational research on the Output Hypothesis by Swain (2005) found that in Canadian immersion programs, the reason some learners failed to achieve native-like proficiency in French was that they did not have sufficient opportunities to use and produce their new language. Language production, as noted earlier in the section about procedural memory, is necessary to develop automaticity (Gass & Mackey, 2015).

Early lessons in adult language programs – for both signed and oral languages – have much in common, typically focusing on greetings, feelings, and introductions. These themes connect with theories of second language acquisition. Conversations about basic topics – introductions, feelings, daily activities, and so on – allow for input, output, and interaction (Gass & Mackey, 2015). Vocabulary can be learned after a single exposure and grammar can be internalized after repeated practice, as the production of one's new language becomes more automated (Ullman, 2015).

Teacher-scholars who have developed signed language curricula adhere to various established learning theories. For example, they tend to avoid grammar-heavy approaches that harken back to when learners were required to translate texts to and from Latin, but never had to *engage in conversation* in their L2 (Finocchiaro & Brumfit, 1983). These teacher-scholars know how adults learn languages and how to teach them to engage in age-peer conversations effectively: they need quality input, opportunities for interaction, and sufficient time for output practice (Gass & Mackey, 2015). For learning a language in a new modality, or M2 (Chen Pichler, 2009), output is especially important because learners need to train their motor system to produce language with their hands, arms, and bodies. This requires repeated trials and "hands-up" time, which helps learners to acquire new motor skills. Through this, their memory systems learn to integrate what they are learning (DeKeyser, 2015; Ullman, 2015).

In addition to the needs of other second language, second modality (L2 M2) learners, families with young deaf children have unique needs (Oyserman & De Geus, 2021a; Snoddon, 2015). While the same theories may underlie any curriculum for this population, families need to learn child-directed language first to fulfill their goal for learning the language: to acquire an L2 and pass it down as a first language (L1) to their child. They are learning the language to expose their deaf child to a fully accessible natural signed language and create a language-rich home environment, a different goal from most other adult L2 learners.

1.1.5 Early Intervention to Improve Language Outcomes

In many countries, deaf children from birth to age three years receive early intervention/early years services to provide early access to language and other developmental areas. These services typically focus on improving the child's language and communication skills, supporting the family's wellbeing and self-efficacy, and facilitating a strong bond between the family and the child (Wright et al., 2021). Research has shown that early identification and intervention are effective in improving the global language skills of young deaf children, regardless of hearing level (Ching et al., 2017; Davidson et al., 2021; Stika et al., 2015).

The earlier deaf children are identified, and their families initiate early intervention services, the greater the children's language development tends to be. In the United States, the American Academy of Pediatrics Joint Committee on Infant Hearing (2019) published principles and guidelines for programs that implement early hearing detection and intervention, specifying what are commonly called the "1–3–6 Guidelines" (Yoshinaga-Itano et al., 2017). These include setting the expectation that all newborn infants have their hearing screened by one month of age, any reduced hearing levels are identified by three months of age, and early intervention services are put in place by six months of age. Yoshinaga-Itano and colleagues (2017) found that infants who met these guidelines had larger vocabularies than infants who did not. Additional variables that accounted for their success in vocabulary acquisition were being younger, not having additional disabilities, having a mild or moderate hearing level, having deaf parents, and having a mother with a higher educational level. According to these findings, although many factors contribute toward higher language outcomes in young deaf children, early identification and intervention play a big role in the process.

Parental involvement is another of these factors. Moeller (2000) measured the vocabulary skills of 112 five-year-old deaf children. They also measured the verbal reasoning skills of eighty of the children, as well as all of their overall language abilities. Finally, they completed a rating scale to measure each child's parents' involvement in the early intervention program that they had attended. The study's results determined that the single most important factor in explaining the children's variance in language skills at five years of age was the level of parental involvement in early intervention (Moeller, 2000). Also, the age at which the child began early intervention was inversely correlated with the child's vocabulary size; that is, the earlier they were enrolled, the larger their vocabulary grew to be. Due to the interactions between the variables, the children with the greatest language outcomes were enrolled early and had highly involved parents. Interestingly, other factors such as degree of hearing loss and nonverbal intelligence were not statistically significant in predicting language outcomes.

1.2 Existing Resources for Early Intervention

Some curricula have been developed to serve families with deaf children in early intervention, such as the *SKI-HI Curriculum*, an American family-centered comprehensive curriculum for early intervention with deaf infants and toddlers (SKI-HI Institute, 2001). The *SKI-HI Curriculum* provides early intervention providers such as teachers of the deaf and deaf mentors with a wide variety of valuable information as families navigate parenting their young children. It includes information about communication opportunities such as signed and oral languages, as well as a wide variety of other topics.

The Central Institute for the Deaf in St. Louis, Missouri, United States (Manley et al., 2019) developed a curriculum titled *Early Listening at Home* (ELH). This is a family-centered curriculum that uses a coaching model for early intervention providers to empower families to support their young deaf child's listening and spoken language. The curriculum includes forty-seven hands-on activities for families to work on their child's early listening skills, as well as many other informative resources about hearing and early listening and language skills. As an orally focused curriculum, ELH's instructional activities do not include strategies to develop children's visual language skills. However, its parent-coaching model is designed to support families in embedding learning activities into daily routines with their children.

It Takes Two to Talk (ITTT, Weitzman, 2017) is a book developed by the Hanen Centre. This Canadian organization provides programs, guidebooks, videos, and workshops for professionals and families of children with language delays and other disabilities to "transform their daily interactions with young children to build the best possible lifelong social, language and literacy skills" (The Hanen Centre, 2019, para. 2). Central to ITTT is instruction on facilitative language techniques that families and professionals can use to support young children's language acquisition. It was developed to support the language needs of children with various disabilities and ITTT briefly mentions that some children use signs or pictures to communicate, but it does not directly address the needs of deaf children. However, the recommendations for families to learn more about their children's communication and implement facilitative language techniques are well-grounded in empirical research (Alper et al., 2021; Barber et al., 2020; Buschmann et al., 2008; Callanan, Signal et al., 2021; Cleave et al., 2015; Ferjan Ramírez et al., 2020; Girolametto et al., 1996, 2016; Kaiser & Hancock, 2003; Kemp & Turnbull, 2014; Rajesh & Venkatesh, 2019; Roberts, 2018; Roberts & Kaiser, 2011; Roberts et al., 2014, 2016). Early intervention providers and families can learn valuable insights from ITTT and other Hanen resources to apply to deaf children's language development.

Callanan and colleagues (Callanan, Ronan et al., 2021; Callanan, Signal et al., 2021) developed a treatment manual for Parent-Child Relationally Informed Early Intervention (PCRI-EI) to develop parent capacities in becoming more attuned to their child, based on the perspective that "child development occurs in the context of the parent-child relationship" (Callanan, Ronan et al., 2021, p. 3). The PCRI-EI manual was developed in Australia to fit a transdisciplinary, clinic-based model. Within that model, the manual walks primary service providers through five phases of parent coaching to build parents' skills and expand their parenting repertoire to support their child's language, cognition, and social-emotional growth. While the PCRI-EI program was not developed specifically for deaf children, it provides a step-by-step guide for early intervention providers to support young children's development by supporting their families.

The SKI-HI Curriculum, ELH, ITTT, and PCRI-EI curricula are valuable resources to support families raising a deaf child. The SKI-HI is a comprehensive support package while ELH focuses specifically on listening skills. Moreover, ITTT and PCRI-EI support the development of any young child receiving early intervention, with ITTT focusing entirely on language development and PCRI-EI covering a wide range of developmental skills.

1.3 Existing Resources for Learning Signed Languages

The focus of this section will be ASL-related resources, as these are more available to us than resources for other signed languages. Where available, other signed language curricula are discussed.

1.3.1 Curricula

Some of the most popular curricula used throughout the United States and Canada are those reviewed by Rosen (2010). They include *Signing Naturally* (Lentz et al., 1992, 2014; Mikos et al., 2001; Smith et al., 2008a); *American Sign Language Phrase Book* (Fant, 1994); *Bravo ASL!* (Cassell & Cox, 1996); *Learning American Sign Language (Levels I and II)* (Humphries & Padden, 2004); and *American Sign Language: Teacher's Resource on Curriculum, Grammar, and Culture and Student Text* (Baker-Shenk & Cokely, 1991). These were written when ASL instruction in high schools and colleges was first gaining popularity. At the time of this publication, ASL is the third most studied language in the United States, after Spanish and French (Looney & Lusin, 2019). More recently, *True+ Way ASL* (Purple Moontower, 2022) has joined these texts in being among the most commonly used in American and Canadian high school and college/ university programs. While the approach to *True+ Way ASL* (TWA) is different from the others in that there is no physical text – everything is online – the purpose of all of these curricula is the same: to teach students to engage with peers of similar age and/or similar college/university standing.

1.3.2 Barriers for Families

Families with young deaf children have very different needs from students who take signed language courses using *Signing Naturally, TWA*, or other curricula developed for secondary and postsecondary instruction. Many traditional ASL courses are cost-prohibitive to families. When classes take place in person, this introduces the additional need for (and cost associated with) childcare. Courses designed for age-peer engagement do not teach the vocabulary or address the communicative situations families of young deaf children face in their everyday lives. The rigor of many courses, especially those at community colleges and universities, is unsuitable for this population. The grandparent of a deaf child who took an ASL class with us based on our family-centered curriculum in January 2021 shared the following about her prior experience in a community education ASL course:

> I took a traditional vocabulary-based class last fall. I only made it through 3 of 10 classes. I dropped out because I was so overwhelmed and felt so incompetent because I couldn't keep up. This [family-centered] class was so

different. The pace was so much better! The videos and GIFs and structure of the class were useful and applicable in everyday life. It made it all seem so achievable and practical and manageable. I will continue to review and practice over and over. And I feel confident that I can look up new vocabulary and slowly add to the base lessons you have provided. The topics are useful every day and most importantly I actually can visualize how this can work now. – *Grandparent of a deaf child. Shared with permission.*

These barriers make traditional classes inaccessible for families with young children. Another key point is that families' primary need for a curriculum is not to be able to engage with age peers, but to be able to engage with their children (Oyserman & De Geus, 2021a; Snoddon, 2015), and most currently available curricula miss the mark.

1.4 Combining Forces for a Family-Centered Curriculum

Sections 1.2 and 1.3 described resources for early intervention, some deaf-specific and some not, and the availability of signed language curricula designed for adult L2 learners. This section will describe how these foci can be modified to create a curriculum that centers the experiences of families of deaf children while providing them with the supportiveness of programs like SKI-HI and ITTT for child-directed signed language instruction.

1.4.1 Who Could Use it, and How?

A family-centered signed language curriculum has a variety of potential uses. Early intervention providers such as teachers of the deaf and deaf mentors/ coaches could use the curriculum to support families' signed language learning during home visits, to provide group classes, or through video conferencing individual or group sessions. In collaboration with these providers, SLPs (or speech-language therapists, as they are called in some countries) could reinforce facilitative language techniques during daily routines. Families could also use the curriculum to learn signed language independently, especially in situations where there are no deaf-specific providers available.

Family involvement in signed language acquisition is paramount (Enns & Price, 2013). To facilitate this, a curriculum designed specifically for the activities families engage in with their deaf infant, toddler, or child has significant appeal. Specifically, rather than learning dozens of words per week that have nothing to do with interacting with a child (e.g., Unit 3 of *Signing Naturally* is all about explaining where the learner lives in relation to their work/school and how to get from place to place; Smith et al., 2008b), families could learn smaller chunks of language at a time that apply directly to activities of daily living.

These could include meals, diaper changing, getting dressed, getting in and out of the car, and getting ready for bed, among many others. In such a curriculum, language learning is reinforced through routine use for both adults and children.

While most of the curricula discussed in this Element focus on ASL, we hope it will have a broader appeal. Actual statistics may vary, but generally speaking, the rate of deafness is roughly the same globally, with slightly higher rates of deafness in developing nations (Haile et al., 2021; Korver et al., 2017; Neumann et al., 2019). As we will describe later in this Element, a family-centered signed language curriculum is, in function, both a second- and first-language acquisition book. It teaches adults – the parents and family members of deaf children – a signed language as an L2, which allows them to provide an accessible environment in which their children can start acquiring that signed language as an L1.

Deaf children from hearing families whose families decide to learn a signed language have much in common with children from immigrant families. Like many immigrant children who learn their region's majority language at school and in the community alongside their parents, these deaf children will likely gain greater proficiency in their L1 than their families will in their L2 (see also Singleton & Newport, 2004 for a case of a deaf child's ASL surpassing his deaf late-signing parents). This is often the case despite families' efforts to learn the language because first language acquisition in early childhood occurs at a much more rapid rate than second language acquisition in adulthood (Lindert, 2001). As families strive to learn as much as possible, it is also valuable to acknowledge this likelihood from the beginning of their signed language learning journey (Napier et al., 2007) as motivation to expose their child to fluent deaf language models as much as possible.

1.4.2 A Case Study of ASL at Home

During the 2020 COVID-19 lockdown, we were stuck at home (together) with only our daily dog walks to get us out of the house. During these walks, we talked about how our lives had been upended by the pandemic. In particular, the first author, an SLP in the school setting, was dealing with major adjustments to his early intervention work. His work included working with parents and families of deaf infants during home visits, as well as serving toddlers and preschoolers directly at school, following two primary therapeutic models. The first, "push-in" therapy, included going into a classroom for deaf children and joining them in their play, letting the child lead as he used facilitative language techniques to improve their language skills in ASL and English. The second, "pull-out" therapy, included bringing children to a designated speech-language therapy room to participate in structured activities to improve their communication skills. When the schools pivoted to distance learning due to the pandemic, direct therapy with toddlers and many preschoolers was not possible; two-year-olds (and many three- and four-year-olds) could not sit still for lessons on Zoom or understand the interactions that took place through a screen. This meant that his job pivoted to include more parent coaching, especially featuring ASL instruction and tips for navigating the journey of raising deaf children and being able to communicate effectively with them at home. His experience confirmed what he had known was needed for years and had searched for without success: a curriculum for families to learn ASL and navigate their journey. He sought out the second author's expertise in second language acquisition and curriculum development and the two authors combined forces to write that much-needed curriculum.

The first edition of the book, titled *American Sign Language at Home: A Family Curriculum* (*ASL at Home*, Zarchy & Geer, 2020) featured three main sections: language instruction (including theme-based vocabulary, fingerspelling, and expressive and receptive sentence practice); facilitative language techniques (which we called "language enrichment techniques") teaching families how to make the most of their interactions with their children and apply the new language skills they had learned to a daily routine; and skills, knowledge, and resources that minoritized communities acquire through lived experiences and can pass down to future generations, also known in this case as Deaf Community Cultural Wealth (Fleischer et al., 2015; Johnson et al., 2020; Yosso, 2005).

ASL at Home (Zarchy & Geer, 2020) had four chapters centered around meal time, bath time, diaper changing, and book sharing, routines that happened multiple times per day or week. The last chapter endeavored to build families' confidence in reading with their young deaf child, even if they were in the earliest stages of learning ASL. These routine-based lessons gave families multiple opportunities to engage with their child using their new language skills by applying a specific language enrichment technique, to improve their retention of those new skills.

From *ASL at Home*'s inception, we welcomed feedback from families and service providers on improving the curriculum. One of the most frequent comments we received was a request for more lessons. In response, we began work on the second edition of *ASL at Home* soon after the first edition was released. The second edition was released in June 2023. Instead of only four chapters, it contains twelve chapters, each based on a young child's routine. The format of the chapters is the same as in the first edition, but many resources have been added, and the instruction is cumulative across the twelve chapters. Additionally, the second edition of *ASL at Home* supports the Deaf Ecosystem (Brick, 2019) by including illustrations, instructional videos, and graphic design by deaf individuals.

We were fortunate to combine our respective skill sets and develop a curriculum grounded in theories and practical applications of first and second language acquisition, family-centered early intervention, parent-implemented communication treatment, and deaf culture. We have received feedback from many families and service providers stating that *ASL at Home* filled a significant gap in family resources. We have also received comments/queries on social media about translation into other signed languages. Based on our experiences with developing and disseminating *ASL at Home*, we recommend that practitioners and scholars in other countries collaborate across disciplines to develop family-centered signed language curricula to match their linguistic and cultural needs and support families in providing early language access for deaf children.

1.5 Roadmap to this Element

Section 2 of this Element will describe families' specific needs, from the journey they experience upon their child's identification as deaf, to why and how families learn signed language successfully. In Section 3, we will describe the recommended components of family-centered signed language curricula, using *ASL at Home* as an example. We will include the evidence in the literature to support each claim. We also provide a detailed tutorial in Appendix A to assist readers with developing their own curricula. In Section 4, we will share the results of survey research on the *ASL at Home* curriculum and introduce potential future directions and improvements based on feedback we have received. Finally, in Section 5, we will conclude with a summary of this Element's claims and recommendations for professionals who endeavor to create family-centered signed language curricula worldwide.

2 The Unique Needs of Families with Deaf Children

2.1 The Family Journey at the Time of Identification

Many countries have implemented universal newborn hearing screening (UNHS) programs to identify all children who are deaf within their first few days of life (Aurélio & Tochetto, 2010; CDC, 2015; Elliott et al., 2022; Moeller et al., 2006; Shearer et al., 2019; Thomson & Yoshinaga-Itano, 2018; Wroblewska-Seniuk et al., 2017). There are two possible outcomes of a screening: "pass," which means the child's hearing levels are likely in the typical range, and "fail," "refer," or "not pass,[2]" which all mean the infant should be re-screened and potentially referred to an audiologist for a diagnostic evaluation. Families in some countries and regions still struggle with a lack of access to hearing screenings, treatment facilities, and listening devices for their children (CDC, 2015; Mostafavi et al., 2017). When a child from a hearing family is first identified as deaf, the family has specific support needs to address any emotional responses they have to the identification; questions they have about supporting their child's needs, particularly concerning communication and language acquisition; and worries they have for their child's future.

Elliot and colleagues (2022) interviewed parents of deaf children about their support needs through the hearing diagnosis pathway of the Victorian Infant Hearing Screening Program (VIHSP) in Victoria, Australia in September 2021, during the statewide lockdown due to the COVID-19 pandemic. During the diagnostic period after the newborn hearing screening, multiple parents reported that professionals told them that their child had probably referred on (not passed) the screening because of fluid in the ears. This frustrated the parents because that (false) reassurance set up an unrealistic expectation that their child was probably hearing and they should not even consider that their child was permanently deaf. Most parents said that they likely would have felt less shocked by the final identification if the individuals doing the screening and post-counseling had explained that there was a chance their child was deaf. They also expressed a wish to take home more information after identification so they could process the information and continue their own learning (see also Rems-Smario, 2017a, for another example of a family wishing for processing time). Similarly, Shezi and Joseph (2021) found that parents of deaf children in South Africa reported a need to know the etiology of their child's reduced hearing because some parents blamed themselves or their spouses for the child's deafness. Thus, clarifying the etiology was important for resolving any such strife in the family. Parents also needed more professional support in obtaining and explaining the individualized information they sought.

The parents in two Australian studies (Elliott et al., 2022; Nickbakht et al., 2019) also expressed that they wished they had received more information about Australian Sign Language, or Auslan. They had difficulty figuring out how to gain that information when the support worker did not provide it

---

[2] Benedict and Stecker (2011) recommend using "refer" rather than "fail" because the latter is negative and suggests a deficit or something inherently wrong with the infant. While this is an important consideration – what message is being given to the parents of a newborn – newer research from the field of audiology suggests that "refer" is not a term families understand. Not understanding the term increases "loss to follow-up," or whether families seek further evaluation after the initial newborn hearing screening. Thus, McAlexander and colleagues (2022) suggest using "not pass" instead.

(see also Matthijs et al., 2017, for similar findings in Flanders). These experiences were consistent with the experiences of parents in Shezi and Joseph's study (2021), in which parents reported that the informational counseling they received from audiologists contained significant gaps in communication strategies, educational options, and communication options, even though those were some of the most highly-sought topics for parents. In particular, 71 percent of parents reported information about signed language classes as a gap in the informational counseling they received (Shezi & Joseph, 2021).

2.1.1 What Signed Language Support Are Families Getting?

The Norwegian program "Se Mitt Språk" (See My Language) is a training program offered to families of deaf children, in which the parents and siblings receive a total of 40 weeks' worth of full-time instruction in Norwegian Sign Language (NSL) with the overall goals of breaking down the language barrier in the family and enabling parents to communicate effortlessly with their children in NSL (Vonen, 2019). The families can take two to four weeks of courses per year until the deaf child is 16 years old. They also learn about deaf culture and history, bilingualism in Norwegian and NSL, and their rights under the National Insurance Scheme and the Education Act.

In South Africa, Maluleke and colleagues (2021) discovered a shift toward family-centered early intervention (FCEI) that was culturally congruent with the family's needs. Caregivers particularly preferred that coaching by early intervention professionals be culturally and linguistically appropriate and sensitive to their time needs. Some of the most challenging aspects of early intervention programs included logistics, challenges specific to the professionals, and challenges specific to the caregivers. For families who want to learn South African Sign Language (SASL), the Department of South African Sign Language and Deaf Studies at the University of the Free State offers a basic SASL Short Learning Program, as well as other SASL workshops and a "Parents with Deaf Children Workshop" (University of the Free State, 2022).

In India, the Early Intervention Project for Deaf Children was launched in April 2018 by the Haryana Welfare Society for Persons with Speech and Hearing Impairment (Vishwakarma & Kulshrestha, 2022). The staff running this project were all deaf and the project was bilingual, focusing on Indian Sign Language and a local spoken language for children ages birth to six years. According to Vishwakarma and Kulrestha's description of the program (2022), it was successful when it began, and they noted significant improvements in the children's receptive and expressive Indian Sign Language skills. However, at the onset of the COVID-19 pandemic, when services had to pivot to an online platform, the program encountered significant barriers due to technical difficulties, large physical distances between the families' homes and the program, and the children's difficulty learning via an online medium. In response to these challenges, the intervention team created videos in Indian Sign Language paired with children's books and other remote resources. Unfortunately, the number of participants in the program decreased from 199 in April 2018 to 29 families in March 2022. As the pandemic abated and educational centers were allowed to reopen, enrollment increased to 155 participants by June 2022. During the worst of the pandemic, the program organizers observed a decline in the participants' Indian Sign Language skills, but their skills began to improve again once the program reopened.

The Irish Department of Education and Skills funds a home-tuition scheme, described by O'Brien (2021), in which families with deaf children can hire teachers to support their learning of Irish Sign Language (ISL). Unfortunately, the scheme has a history of low pay for ISL teachers, lack of advertising, and low overall usage by families, often due to a lack of information. A Visiting Teacher Service (VTS) is also available to families from preschool to third level to support the child's development (Mathews, 2011).

In the United Kingdom, every child identified as deaf by the universal newborn hearing screening program is contacted by a Qualified Teacher of the Deaf (sometimes one with an early years specialization), who supports the family through the child's preschool period. Early intervention teams use a variety of interventions, such as parent-implemented communication treatment (PICT), the Muenster Parenting Program, an intervention program based on the empowerment of mothers, auditory-verbal therapy, and more (Wright et al., 2021).

As part of a larger ethnographic research project to explore Francophone hearing parents of deaf children's experiences in Canada, Switzerland, France, and Belgium, Puyaltó and colleagues (2018) found that many families reported long waiting lists when they attempted to access early intervention, audiological, or speech and language services. Even when assigned to specialists, parents were often displeased with the professional's competency level in working with deaf children. They described their experiences with the system as a "constant battle" (p. 8) and learned to advocate for their deaf children to obtain their needed support.

2.1.2 Tools Families Use to Learn Signed Languages

Decker and Vallotton (2016) interviewed hearing parents of deaf children in Michigan, United States to identify themes in the information they received from early intervention service providers. Some – not all – of the parents received information about adding signs to speech with their child, but commented that the information they received was infrequent and incomplete. They primarily received small booklets or referrals to websites but did not receive information about learning a complete signed language to communicate with their child. As noted in Section 2.1, the same has been noted of families seeking resources for learning Auslan and Flemish Sign Language (Elliott et al., 2022; Matthijs et al., 2017; Nickbakht et al., 2019). Family-centered signed language curricula have been developed for some signed languages including Norwegian Sign Language (Vonen, 2019), Sign Language of the Netherlands (Oyserman & De Geus, 2021b), and German Sign Language (Kestner, 2021).

When Lieberman and colleagues (2022) surveyed parents of deaf children on their ASL skills and resources they used to learn the language, formal ASL classes were ranked as the most useful resource, whether at the college level or through their child's school or early intervention program. Organizations such as the American Society for Deaf Children (ASDC), local community organizations, and early intervention programs sometimes offer signed language classes for families and the broader community. For example, Advancement in Sign Language Education and Services (Asles) provides virtual, hybrid, and in-person courses at different levels, based in San Juan, Puerto Rico.

The same investigation showed that the next most useful resource for parents' ASL learning was self-teaching using various sources such as apps, television shows, YouTube videos, dictionaries, and websites with child-specific ASL content (Lieberman et al., 2022). When they compared the parents' self-ratings of ASL skills across learning resources, the parents who had taken a formal ASL class and those who had informal interactions with deaf adults ranked their skills slightly higher than others, but the findings were overall similar across resources. Many parents stated that they did not believe there were enough resources available for hearing families to learn ASL.

Families of deaf children often seek signed language dictionaries to teach themselves signs to use with their children. However, many parents recognize that single signs are not sufficient to communicate effectively and express the desire to learn how to string signs together into full sentences (Decker & Vallotton, 2016). In the first author's clinical experience, families learn many ASL words independently, but those words are predominantly nouns and pre-academic vocabulary words such as colors, animals, and vehicles. In these situations, families report that although they know many signs, they still do not know enough of the signed language itself to communicate with their child in sentences and conversations. A study by Banajee and colleagues (2003) demonstrated that the most frequently used words for toddlers included non-noun word classes, such as pronouns, verbs, prepositions, and demonstratives.

These are words that can be used across a variety of pragmatic functions, such as requesting, affirming, and negating. Nouns were conspicuously absent from this list. The results of this study are significant because it is during the toddler age that most children begin to combine words into sentences. They and their families require a diverse vocabulary across word classes to communicate effectively with each other. For example, participants in a recent study by Oyserman and de Geus in the Netherlands wanted a course "similar to learning English as an L2 ... to communicate with their deaf child [and] achieve parent-child pedagogical communication skills to the fullest extent possible" (Oyserman & de Geus, 2021a, p. 179). The first author recalls many parents of deaf children who have told him, "I know so many signs, but I still don't know how to talk to my child!"

Some early intervention programs provide deaf mentors as a related service under the Individualized Family Service Plan (Abrams & Gallegos, 2011). Interacting with deaf mentors and other members of the deaf community is very beneficial to families of deaf children, who report appreciation for the support they receive from the community (Lieberman et al., 2022) and for the perspective they gain on who their child may grow up to become (Crace et al., 2022; Gale et al., 2021). Involving deaf adults in early intervention satisfies two of the Best Practice Principles included in the International Consensus Statement developed by a diverse panel of experts in Bad Ischl, Austria in 2012 (Moeller et al., 2013): Principle 4 (social and emotional support for families from adult role models who are deaf and hard of hearing) and Principle 8 (early intervention transdisciplinary teams). These principles state that best practices for early intervention include support for families from deaf adults and collaboration with deaf adults in various roles throughout the early intervention system. When families interact with deaf adults early in their child's life, they learn that their child may be different from them, but they are not broken (Hamilton & Clark, 2020). Soon after deaf mentors were first introduced in Utah, United States, a study compared deaf children in that state who had deaf mentors with children in Tennessee who did not. Researchers found that children with deaf mentors made greater progress in social, cognitive, and language development (Watkins et al., 1998). Unfortunately, some early intervention programs only provide deaf mentors until the child turns three years old and transitions from an Individualized Family Service Plan (IFSP) to an Individualized Education Plan (IEP, IDEA, 2004). At this point, the focus of services shifts from the whole family to the child's educational environment.

In the state of New Mexico in the United States, the Deaf Role Model Program serves deaf children and their families statewide as a recognized early intervention service provided by the New Mexico School for the Deaf (Abrams, 2014; Abrams & Gallegos, 2011). The providers live in the same communities as the families they serve, so they are familiar with the local culture and traditions. In addition to providing families with aspirational capital by seeing who their child could become and sharing their own stories with families,[3] deaf role models in this program teach ASL to families and show them how to make their child's world more accessible. They also use the *SKI-HI Curriculum* (SKI-HI Institute, 2001) to address the myriad other aspects of early intervention and raising a deaf child.

We are most familiar with online resources available for families to learn ASL, though there may be equivalent resources for other signed languages. One online resource for families to learn ASL is called *SignOn*, a "virtual immersion tool" that connects learners with Deaf Ambassadors in online, 30-minute one-on-one virtual sessions (*SignOn*, 2022). *SignOn* offers flexible scheduling at descending costs depending on the number of sessions purchased. *SignOn* has an agreement with the American Society for Deaf Children (ASDC, 2022) through which ASDC members can get five free 30-minute *SignOn* sessions. *SignOn* also has recommendations for how to include *SignOn* services on a child's IEP or IFSP (*SignOn*, 2022).

Many families turn to social media when their signed language learning needs are not fully met by classes, dictionaries, apps, and other resources, or as a supplement to their other learning. There are many social media accounts created specifically to teach ASL, as well as to get the word out about deaf-led signed language classes and to spread knowledge about being deaf. Some examples include the Instagram accounts of Loni Friedman (@loni.friedmann), who describes herself as a "Functional ASL DeafBlind Queer Instructor," and Sara Miller, MSEd (@adventuresindeafed), who describes herself as an "Advocate for the Deaf community, accessibility, inclusion, and equity." For Australian Sign Language (Auslan), two popular accounts belong to Melissa Bryson (@auslanrocks), a "Deaf Mum/Nana of 2 Deaf daughters & 3 Deaf grandsons. Teacher of the Deaf/Tutor, Auslan lecturer" and David Grant (@auslanwithdavid), a "Deaf actor, YouTuber, and Auslan user."

YouTube videos are also a common resource for families. Some YouTube channels commonly recommended among parents of deaf children include songs and television shows on MyGo's channel (Moonbug Entertainment, 2022) and the signed children's literature on Rocky Mountain Deaf School's channel (Rocky Mountain Deaf School, 2022). The ASDC also has an ASL Stories Directory, which links to videos of deaf adults signing a vast collection of children's literature (ASDC, 2022).

---

[3] A type of cultural wealth that refers to the ability to maintain one's hopes and dreams in the face of real or perceived barriers (Fleischer et al., 2015; Johnson et al., 2020; Yosso, 2005).

2.2 Why Some Families Learn Sign Language

Most hearing families of deaf children do not learn a signed language. In fact, according to the Gallaudet Research Institute's report from 2013 to 2014, only 22.9 percent of American families with deaf children sign regularly at home (Office of Research Support and International Affairs, 2014). The early hearing detection and intervention (EHDI) process does not necessarily facilitate families' learning and finding resources about signed language. In a study of 100 parents conducted across the United States, only one-fourth of parents with deaf children learned about ASL from their early intervention providers, and very few learned about it from healthcare professionals such as pediatricians or audiologists (Lieberman et al., 2022).

For deaf children, in particular, families often report receiving conflicting information from early intervention providers regarding the "best" communication opportunities to use with their child (Lillo-Martin et al., 2021). With the advent of technologies such as cochlear implants and digital hearing aids, many deaf children have more access to sound and oral language than was previously possible, so some families choose an approach that includes only listening and spoken language (LSL). However, technological advances such as cochlear implantation do not solve the problem of language deprivation because the oral language outcomes for implanted children remain highly varied. Some evidence points to early initiation of early intervention services (Yoshinaga-Itano et al., 2017), early entrance into a signing school for the deaf (Henner et al., 2016), early cochlear implantation (Duchesne & Marschark, 2019), and early language progress on outcomes such as mean length of utterance (Szagun & Schramm, 2016) as factors contributing to later language success. However, it is not yet possible to predict which children will successfully acquire oral language (Niparko et al., 2010) and the evidence base for oral-only approaches such as auditory-verbal therapy (AVT) remains weak (Kaipa & Danser, 2016). Additionally, oral deaf children with cochlear implants continue to underperform in their language skills compared to hearing children (Lund, 2016; Niparko et al., 2010).

Groups of professionals have recommended a default early intervention protocol for deaf children that uses a bimodal bilingual approach; that is, an approach that includes both a natural signed language and an oral/written language to prevent language deprivation (Clark et al., 2020). Recent research in parent use of signed language in the home is also promising: Caselli and colleagues (2021) found that deaf children whose parents began learning ASL by the time the child was six months old had age-appropriate vocabularies by the time they turned two years old.

Professionals designing classes for hearing families of deaf children must remember that these families have unique needs that are distinct from those of other adults who take signed language classes. They need to learn language skills that they can apply directly to communication and bonding with their children, with opportunities to practice at home (Oyserman & De Geus, 2021a). When they do, they can leverage their new skills to achieve successful communication with their children (Harris & Mohay, 1997). As opposed to college students who take a more typical language course to meet foreign language requirements, or due to interest in the subject, families of deaf children take signed language classes out of necessity (Napier et al., 2007) to satisfy their immediate communication needs at home.

Dutra (2020) investigated the motivations, barriers, and facilitators that influenced hearing parents of deaf children to learn ASL in California, United States. The primary motivations that drove parents to learn ASL included the need to communicate with their children, to teach their children, to see their children succeed, to be good parents, and to have relationships with their children. There were many barriers to language learning, including time, the learning curve of the language, others' perceptions of them and their families, and their own internal conflicts. Facilitating factors for their signed language learning included having a strong support system and inner strengths such as grit and faith. The findings of that study led to Dutra's development of parent acceptance theory (PAT, Dutra, 2020). According to PAT, accepting their unique circumstances, including their child's deafness, facilitates parents' ability to overcome barriers, use resources, and seek out the support networks they need. PAT also shows that the process of accepting their deaf child made it possible for parents to learn a natural signed language and appreciate the richness that having that child added to their life.

3 The Components of a Family-Centered Curriculum

The previous sections have demonstrated the urgency for parents and families of deaf children to learn a signed language. They also explained how adults learn a second language and described the unique learning needs of families. Traditional signed language curricula for adults, while important resources, are often not suitable (first) curricula for families with young deaf children. To address this, we propose developing family-centered curricula. But what components are key in this type of curriculum? The following subsections detail this, using *American Sign Language at Home* (*ASL at Home*, Zarchy and Geer, 2020, 2023) as an example, and give a rationale for each component's inclusion.

3.1 Routine-Based Vocabulary Structure

Routine-based language learning refers to selecting a routine common in daily life and learning words and linguistic structures to discuss that routine. For the adults in a young child's life, this means selecting those routines that are common in the child's life and offer opportunities for engagement between adult and child. This is why a curriculum focused not on adult-to-adult communication, but on adult-to-child, or child-directed communication (and when the child is old enough, child-to-adult communication as well) is so critical. The next three subsections describe the evidence-based rationale for embedding language intervention into daily routines, how this relates to incidental learning, and how to use daily routines to select appropriate, accessible vocabulary to teach in a family-centered curriculum.

3.1.1 Intervention Is Most Effective When Embedded in Daily Routines

Best practices in early intervention are centered around home-based supports in daily routines (Hintermair, 2016; McWilliam, 2016; Quiñonez Summer, 2022; Sass-Lehrer et al., 2016), which centers the family as the unit of attention (Sass-Lehrer et al., 2016). This approach sets up early intervention providers to follow a set of values established for early intervention in the United States (Quiñonez Summer, 2022), including providing services to children and families through daily routines, working with families in a family-friendly way, and focusing on family quality of life (Hintermair, 2016; McWilliam, 2010b).

The five practices needed to implement these values in the everyday lives of families are "assessing informal and formal supports, assessing functional needs in everyday situations, coordinating services, using home visits to provide support, and consulting collaboratively with childcare providers" (Hintermair, 2016, p. 2). To implement these practices, particularly those of assessing functional needs in everyday situations and using home visits to provide support, best practices for early intervention include providing family-centered signed language instruction in a functional manner that makes families feel comfortable in their natural environment, embedded in family routines (Gallegos et al., 2016). Providers can conduct a routines-based interview to determine the family's functional needs (McWilliam, 2010a), and then identify natural opportunities for families to incorporate their learning into everyday life. It is especially beneficial to embed new learning into activities that happen multiple times per day, such as eating, diapering, and going places (Gallegos et al., 2016). To achieve that end, signed language instruction for families is most effective when it teaches adults the skills necessary to communicate with children during these daily routines (Napier et al., 2007).

Because children learn best from caregivers in their natural environment, many early intervention professionals provide services through parent coaching. Parent coaching describes the process by which a service provider passes on information and skills to a child's caregiver, who then implements the intervention strategies with the child. Under the parent-coaching model, rather than early intervention providers working with children, they "work with adults *about* children" (McWilliam, 2016, p. 180). Children learn more through their daily encounters and experiences than they do through repeated trials in a short period of time (McWilliam, 2016); thus, when providers teach families to apply intervention strategies, the families can use those strategies throughout the day and week, providing their child with rich learning experiences without depending on the presence of a provider to do so.

This parent-coaching framework necessitates that providers follow the family's lead to learn about their daily routines, and then embed intervention into them. When providers teach through routines, they are encouraging parent–child interaction (Enns & Price, 2013) and language, which fosters the development of the whole child (Lytle & Oliva, 2016). Interaction brings about learning in two key ways: through negotiating for meaning and through interactional adjustments (Gass & Mackey, 2015). As the child starts to produce language independently, the adult and child can work together to ensure mutual understanding. This two-way interaction achieves four aims: It pushes *output* opportunities for the adult (Pannell et al., 2017) while giving the child *input*, and then gives the adult *input* opportunities while pushing the child's *output*. What this further suggests is that families should be encouraged to interact with their children and allow for the crucial *input, interaction,* and *output* (Gass & Mackey, 2015) described in Section 1.1.4. These interactions and opportunities for language use and development will feed the cycle of communication between adults and children.

3.1.2 Incidental Learning Through Routines: Fostering Multilingualism within the Family

The declarative/procedural model, discussed in Section 1.1.4, is a neurobiologically motivated theory of first and second language acquisition. This model assumes that language skills like vocabulary are learned quickly through declarative memory, and skills like grammar are slower to be learned because they require prolonged practice. This relates to fostering bi- or multilingualism within the family.

One important reason for fostering learning through routines is to ensure that children have access to language in their ambient environment, not only when they are being addressed directly. Incidental, or contextual, learning combines background knowledge and current context to form meaning from informal interactions in the surrounding environment. This type of learning, which is unplanned and results from access to the ambient environment, is often inaccessible to deaf children in hearing families. However, signed conversations between others in the home can improve that access (Hopper, 2011; Lane et al., 1996). Children commonly learn vocabulary without someone intentionally teaching it to them because they can pick up new words through watching the accessible signed conversations between others. For example, suppose a parent of two children was conversing with the older child about getting ready for school. The baby might be able to make correct form–meaning pairings for tokens like "backpack," "shoes," or perhaps "jacket," as these are all likely to come up in this sort of conversation.

This relates to the work of Napier and colleagues (2007), who found that in the home of a deaf child, "[o]ther family members also need to learn sign language so that the language really is the language of the home. If parents can sign, but siblings or other extended family cannot, then the deaf child will miss out on much of the incidental learning that happens by 'overhearing' the conversations of other people" (p. 87). Indeed, in a video produced by Gallaudet University, scholars stress that the language environment for deaf children should be accessible, interactive, and abundant. Part of that "abundance" is ensuring that everyone in the child's environment is using an accessible language, allowing the child to continue pattern-seeking as they decode their first language and make form–meaning pairings (Simms et al., 2016).

When deaf children have access to language in their home, they can acquire the family's home culture, whatever it may be, because the family can explain routines, customs, and rituals to the child. When demonstrating "how we do things," language permits adults and older children to teach young children the what, where, when, why, and how of their family's culture. Celina, the mother of a deaf child, noted that "even if [her children] didn't respond back, I know that my number one priority was giving them a language they could access and they could use so they knew I loved them" (Rems-Smario, 2017b, 1:50–2:00). Celina went on to describe her ASL-learning journey: "One thing that a teacher told me, was I was struggling with language with my kids, and . . . they said: 'well, even if they don't respond right away, keep signing, all the time, around them. Even if it's just one word in a sentence, sign it, and your language is gonna expand'" (Rems-Smario, 2017b, 2:18–2:30). This relates to the input, output, and interaction theory because the adult is seizing every opportunity to apply the routine-specific signs and structures they have learned to various daily routine interactions, which are L2 output opportunities. This, in turn, gives the child both direct and incidental L1 input.

3.1.3 Vocabulary Selection

Family-centered curricula, in addition to teaching child-directed language, must consider the audience of learners and consider how many words the child's family can learn and retain per lesson. Another crucial factor in choosing vocabulary words is whether (and how) those words can be immediately made into sentences that can be used throughout a daily routine. Readers may recall from Section 1.1.4 that adult learners arrive at the task of language learning knowing that languages have words (VanPatten, 2015). By carefully selecting words that families can learn in isolation and then learn to recognize in context, learners will become more successful with parsing the signed language stream. Families should feel capable of learning a signed language, but if the curriculum is too rigorous, this may not be the case. When Lieberman and colleagues (2022) surveyed hearing parents who learned ASL to communicate with their deaf children, many parents reported that they felt "overwhelmed, embarrassed, discouraged or frustrated" while learning (p. 16). However, those who were able to overcome those feelings found the learning process to be worthwhile. Thus, *ASL at Home* chapters contain only eight to twelve words each.

The vocabulary covered in *ASL at Home* mostly includes core vocabulary, as opposed to fringe vocabulary. "Core vocabulary" refers to a relatively small collection of the most commonly used words (Yorkston et al., 1988). "Fringe vocabulary" refers to words that are used in specific activities or environments, such as words for varieties of foods or animals (Banajee et al., 2003). In a study of hearing English-speaking children, just 100 words made up 71 percent of the vocabulary they used daily at school (Boenisch & Soto, 2015). Even for school-aged children, a great deal of life's communication requires only a small number of particularly useful words.

Nouns make up a large portion of toddlers' vocabularies. However, their most frequently used word tokens are pronouns, verbs, prepositions, and demonstratives (Banajee et al., 2003). This variety of word types is much easier to combine into sentences than a list of nouns. Also, nouns are some of the easiest words to locate in dictionaries, since it is often clear exactly which word is needed. For example, if a parent is reading a book to their child about a giraffe but does not yet know the ASL word for "giraffe," a dictionary search for the word "giraffe" would be helpful. However, it might not be as obvious that the word "ready" would be helpful when asking if the child is ready to turn the page, or indeed how to say "turn the page." For this reason, we recommend choosing core vocabulary as the majority of the words taught in a family-centered curriculum, and then giving families resources to look up any additional words they need to communicate with their child and continue developing their language proficiency.

3.2 Language Practice

The previous section explains the role of theme-based learning with core vocabulary and how to embed this in daily routines. However, language learning is so much more than vocabulary alone. To acquire language, children need to see others use language more advanced than their own (Boyce et al., 2013). Communication takes place through utterances containing variably fixed multi-word expressions that people recycle and use as building blocks to construct more complex utterances in both signed and oral languages (Wilkinson et al., 2023). By teaching families of deaf children to produce multi-word expressions, the *ASL at Home* curriculum provides them with these building blocks, which they can learn to manipulate and "recycle" as their vocabulary and familiarity with the language increases. The remainder of this section details how grammar is introduced in *ASL at Home* and how it fits with various theories of second language acquisition discussed previously. The key here is that families need to learn *functional* grammar as it comes up through daily routines, in order to push them beyond using only single words in their output without overwhelming them.

3.2.1 Grammar in ASL at Home

The main goal of *ASL at Home* is not to teach grammar, necessarily, but to give families functional communication and language during the most critical period of language acquisition for their young children. That said, the curriculum does include some grammar instruction in small doses, specifically where it becomes relevant and functional for making sentences. For example, several agreement verbs (verbs that change direction depending on the subject and object of the verb) are taught throughout the curriculum, starting in chapter 1 (Meal Time). A breakout box in that chapter provides an explanation of what agreement verbs are, how they behave, and what this means functionally for forming sentences. With this, learners are exposed to the grammatical concept and provided with repeated opportunities to use what they have learned, both in the sentence practice sections of the curriculum (expressive and receptive) and in the language enrichment techniques section. Here, learners are asked to think about what they would say in a given scenario using the facilitative language technique of the week. These output opportunities can lead to corrections and refinement in their productions when families use the curriculum in a virtual *Learn ASL at Home* class with us, a class provided by an organization or school district that has adopted the curriculum as part of their early intervention program, or home-based early intervention services with a teacher of the deaf or deaf mentor.

Another breakout box in chapter 2 (Bath Time) of *ASL at Home* teaches about classifiers. This is an especially important lesson because many people still misunderstand ASL as "English on the hands" (and other natural signed languages as manual forms of the majority spoken language in the area) and expect a one-to-one correspondence for each English word in manual form. As this is not the case, and one of the places this is the most apparent is when classifiers are used, it is important to explain what classifiers are and how they can be used. Additionally, because classifiers are an important part of storytelling and other rich description in signed languages (Asmal & Kaneko, 2020; Cook, 2011), but signed language learners often struggle to learn them effectively (Chen Pichler, 2021; Chen Pichler et al., 2021), early introduction to classifiers allows families to start getting comfortable with them early in their learning process.

A final example of grammar instruction in the curriculum is a breakout box about pronouns. The second author has been teaching ASL for over ten years and has noted that a common challenge with ASL learners is differentiating between personal and possessive pronouns and that (impressionistically) if this distinction is not learned early, it becomes increasingly difficult to learn. To address this early in the learning process, Zarchy and Geer (2023) teach this in chapter 2. Another benefit to teaching pronouns early is that they are a common type of core vocabulary for toddlers (Banajee et al., 2003) and can be used to form a wide variety of sentences and to increase the length of sentences.

The *ASL at Home* curriculum and virtual *Learn ASL at Home* classes are aligned with the declarative/procedural model. Learners are first exposed to vocabulary and then they practice sentences in various ways. In the expressive sentence practice section of the curriculum, students copy the motor pattern of someone else's signed utterances, not worrying about comprehension. After producing the sentence together as a group several times to enable procedural memory to make the process of producing signs more automatic, learners are asked about comprehension. However, this is a secondary task of the activity. Another part of the curriculum in which learners can engage procedural memory is during the language enrichment technique lesson. We present various scenarios taking place during the chapter's routine theme, and then participants are asked to come up with ways to apply that chapter's technique and generate new sentences independently (or with support from the class) using the

IXchild	DON'T-LIKE	IXchild	DON'T-WANT	MORE	IXfood	GROSS

"You don't like it?"   *"You don't want more?"*   *"That (food) is gross!"*

Figure 1 Still images of a signer producing the ASL sentences, "IXchild DON'T-LIKE. IXchild DON'T-WANT MORE. IXfood GROSS," meaning, "You don't like it? You don't want more. That (food) is gross." See the original video at bit.ly/zg_video.

vocabulary they have learned. For example, using parallel talk, which is the technique introduced in chapter 1: Meal Time, one of the scenarios reads, "Your child takes a bite of food, then makes a 'yucky' face" (p. 20). In this scenario, learners can draw on what they have learned in the chapter and come up with sentences like the one pictured in Figure 1 meaning, "You don't like it? You don't want more. That (food) is gross."

3.2.2 Learning a Second Language in a Second Modality

Both families of deaf children and pre-service signed language students intending to become interpreters or teachers of the deaf are usually learning a language in the manual modality for the first time. Researchers refer to these learners as L2 M2 – second language, second modality – learners and note that this new modality presents additional considerations for instruction (Chen Pichler, 2009; De Meulder, 2019; Oyserman & De Geus, 2021a). The skill acquisition theory of language (DeKeyser, 2015) provides a framework for understanding why it is important to encourage the use of full sentences as early as possible in the learning process. This theory applies to the learning of any motor skill and posits that there are three stages: cognitive, associative, and autonomous (DeKeyser, 2015). This progression is related to the differing amounts of knowledge one has about a skill at particular stages of learning and the cognitive load associated with producing the skill in a particular stage.

In the cognitive stage, one needs knowledge about a skill before using it; through observation and/or explanation from a teacher, learners are able to attempt the performance of the new skill. For example, for L2 M2 learners, certain formational parameters of signs are more difficult to learn than others. In order of difficulty, the handshape of a sign is the most difficult, followed by its movement, orientation, and location (Ortega & Morgan, 2015). To compensate for learners' difficulty learning handshapes, in instructional videos for vocabulary, the *ASL at Home* language model often demonstrates the handshape before – or sandwiched between – demonstrations of the entirety of a particular sign, as the handshape may be difficult to discern without explicit instruction. In *Learn ASL at Home* classes, our demonstration of signs often includes an explanation of how to produce them. A good example of this is the sign meaning "delicious" or "yummy." This is a motorically difficult sign to produce that requires several step-by-step demonstrations in which we narrate how each aspect of the sign is produced. We might say something like, "start with a 5 handshape, then place your thumb on the first knuckle of your middle finger. Place this at your chin. Slide your thumb down your middle finger to the spot between the first and second knuckles. As you do so, move the hand away from your chin." Production of this sign requires high cognitive effort as learners work their way through its production until the sign becomes more automated. Figure 2 shows a still image representation of how this sign is depicted in *ASL at Home* supplementary learning materials.

For an example of explicit handshape instruction in *ASL at Home* vocabulary instructional videos, see Figure 3.

With repeated practice of individual signs and, importantly, signs in sentences, learners develop a level of proceduralization in which they no longer need to retrieve the individual steps, like those narrated for "delicious" above, of how to form a sign/sentence from memory and reassemble them. Instead, the "program" needed to execute a sign/sentence is readily available and can be deployed at will (DeKeyser, 2015) and with increasing consistency and accuracy; this is the associative stage. With increased practice, there continues to be decreasing cognitive demand in producing the skill and learners can even start

Figure 2 Still image of the ASL sign meaning "delicious." A video of this sign is available at bit.ly/zg_delicious.

Sign demonstration   Handshape demonstration   Sign demonstration

Figure 3 Explicit handshape instruction for the ASL sign meaning "thin,"
sandwiched between still images of the sign. See a video of
this sign here: bit.ly/zg_thin.

to detect and eliminate their own errors (Coker, 2022). To develop this type of
motor program for sign production, learners need to have many trials of
practice, especially with stringing signs together into sentences rather than
producing them in isolation. Ultimately, as learners engage with their young
deaf child, the default becomes to make a sentence rather than a single sign.
Again, following the skill acquisition theory, this repeated practice (also related
to procedural memory) leads to automatization, or producing language without
(or with very little) cognitive effort (i.e., the autonomous stage).

In addition to learning different functions for using signed language in daily
routines and tackling the challenges of motor skill learning, Goodwin and
colleagues (2019) found that learning and producing sentences early in learning
is essential because as a mother's signing becomes more complex, so too does
the child's. All of this suggests that learning *functional* grammar is important for
helping learners become comfortable with producing signs and making the
output process more automated, thus improving the child's input and the quality
of the interaction and ultimately improving the child's sign language skills as
well.

3.2.3 Fluency Outcomes of a Family-Centered Curriculum

The primary goal of a family curriculum is to achieve (at a minimum) a basic
level of language use (Council of Europe, 2022b). According to the Common
European Framework of Reference for Languages (CEFR guidelines), beginning learners should be able to "understand and use familiar everyday expressions and very basic phrases aimed at the satisfaction of needs of a concrete

type," "interact in a simple way," and "understand sentences and frequently used expressions related to areas of most immediate relevance (e.g. very basic personal and family information ...)" (level A1). Learners at level A2 "communicate in simple and routine tasks requiring a simple and direct exchange of information on familiar and routine matters" (Council of Europe, 2022a). This would most closely correspond to the novice-mid or novice-high level from the American Council on the Teaching of Foreign Languages (*ACTFL Proficiency Guidelines 2012*, 2012) because beginning learners are limited to a short list of "everyday topics which affect them directly" (p. 9).

As Blanco (2020) writes, "[l]earning a language doesn't have to mean learning *everything* [emphasis ours] in the language you're studying" (para 1). The same is true for families of deaf children, especially at the earliest stages of learning. While the ability to converse about a wide range of topics will hopefully be the eventual goal, in the beginning, a family-centered curriculum needs to give learners the confidence to get started. Humphries and colleagues (2016) stress that deaf children should be exposed to good language models regularly such as in school, playgroups, or other deaf events with plentiful deaf adult role models. These language models can help reinforce what the child is learning at home. Crucially, it is vital for family members to have a basic level of communication to develop healthy family relationships and encourage the development of the whole deaf child through language (Lytle & Oliva, 2016).

3.3 Language Techniques

The previous two sections described the need for routine-based language instruction for families of deaf children. This section will continue the discussion of the components of a family-centered signed language curriculum by describing the importance of teaching families specific techniques they can use to create a language-rich home. Parent-implemented communication treatment (PICT) is a powerful evidence-based approach in early intervention to improve young children's receptive and expressive language skills (Roberts & Kaiser, 2011). In PICT, a service provider teaches families strategies to improve their abilities to provide a language-rich environment for their children (Wright et al., 2021). The strategies most beneficial to a family-centered signed language curriculum include facilitative language techniques commonly used by SLPs, visual and joint attention language techniques commonly used by deaf families who sign with their children, and the strategic use of techniques to bolster families' self-efficacy and confidence. The next three subsections provide detailed information on these strategies.

3.3.1 Facilitative Language Techniques

Techniques that teach families to create a more language-rich environment have been shown to be effective in increasing language skills in children with a wide variety of disabilities (Barber et al., 2020; Blackwell et al., 2015; Buschmann et al., 2008; O'Toole et al., 2021; Roberts & Kaiser, 2011). Many studies have shown the effectiveness of teaching language techniques to hearing parents of deaf children to improve the children's oral language outcomes (e.g., Brock & Bass-Ringdahl, 2021; Costa et al., 2019; Lund, 2018; Nicastri et al., 2021; Roberts, 2018). However, there is little to no literature on PICT that focuses on improving children's signed language outcomes. This section provides a non-exhaustive list of facilitative language techniques that have been shown to improve deaf children's oral language skills, suggesting that they are also likely to improve deaf children's signed language skills.

DesJardin (2006) described two types of facilitative language techniques: higher-level and lower-level techniques. The most common lower-level language techniques include closed-ended questions, linguistic mapping, directives, and imitations. Brock and Bass-Ringdahl (2021) provided descriptions of these techniques. Linguistic mapping describes interactions in which a child vocalizes or expresses a gestural utterance that is not recognizable as a word. The parent responds by interpreting that utterance into a word. For example, if the child vocalizes and points to a ball, the parent responds by saying "Ball." Directives include interactions in which the parent tells the child to do something or prevents them from doing something. Imitations include the parent directly imitating the child's utterance.

These lower-level language techniques may support the language skills of children in the earlier stages of language development or who have more severe language delays, but they are less effective than high-level techniques (DesJardin, 2004; DesJardin & Eisenberg, 2007). DesJardin (2004) and DesJardin and Eisenberg (2007) found that hearing families of deaf toddlers tended to use fewer utterances and more directive language than families of hearing children. For example, the parents often took control of the conversation, focusing on the child's oral language and disregarding nonverbal communication that the child produced spontaneously. In these situations, families tried to direct the child's attention rather than following the child's attention. For families whose children exhibited communication delays, this increased directiveness may have been a compensatory mechanism to accommodate the child's reduced language skills or to address the mismatch in communication skills between parent and child (Costa et al., 2019). However, excessive parental control of conversations is negatively related to children's acquisition of language skills (Ambrose et al., 2015; Su & Roberts, 2019), so families stand to benefit from learning other communication approaches that are more likely to facilitate their child's language acquisition.

Higher-level language techniques can also be described as conversational eliciting techniques. The most commonly used higher-level techniques include parallel talk (narration), open-ended questions, expansions, and recasts (Brock & Bass-Ringdahl, 2021; DesJardin, 2004; DesJardin & Eisenberg, 2007; Sultana et al., 2019). According to Brock and Bass-Ringdahl (2021), parallel talk describes talking about whatever is holding the child's attention. For example, if the child looks out the window at a garbage truck, the parent could say, "You see the garbage truck!" Expansions are interactions in which the child expresses an utterance that is short or lacks complete grammar. The parent repeats that utterance, adding words or morphemes to make the grammar more complete or to make the sentence longer. For example, if the child says in English, "Him need juice," the adult may respond, "Yes, he needs juice!" Recasts resemble expansions but include rephrasing the child's utterance, changing its voice or perspective, or rephrasing it as a question. For example, if the child says, "Him need juice," the parent may respond with a question like "Does he need some juice?" (Cleave et al., 2015).

In addition to improving parent–child interactions and promoting deaf children's language skills, PICT also empowers families to connect with their children positively by reducing negative talk and directiveness. Some studies have found that deaf children exhibit a higher prevalence of socio-emotional behavioral issues than hearing children, possibly due to difficulties with communication (Hintermair, 2006; Zaidman-Zait, 2008). By giving families a greater understanding of their child's development and communication needs, PICT provides strategies to increase positive parenting. This supports their bonding with their child and teaches them the tools to improve their children's behavior and socio-emotional wellness as well as their language (Costa et al., 2019).

Parent coaching on facilitative language techniques is a common practice in early intervention, particularly in services provided by SLPs and teachers of the deaf. By including these techniques in signed language curricula, curriculum developers provide a prime opportunity for early intervention providers to come together as an interdisciplinary team to support deaf children's language acquisition by supporting their families.

3.3.2 Visual and Joint Attention Language Techniques

Studies of deaf parents reveal that they use techniques specific to the visual modality that can inform how hearing families interact with their deaf children (e.g., Koester & Lahti-Harper, 2010; Spencer, 2001). The visual, tactile, and attention-getting techniques that deaf parents naturally use with their children appear to foster greater visual and attentional skills. Thus, if hearing parents with deaf children implement these techniques, they may achieve greater congruence between their communication and that of their child. For example, deaf children with deaf parents tend to have higher levels of gaze-following behavior than hearing children with hearing parents (Brooks et al., 2020) and deaf parents tend to be more responsive than hearing parents are to toddlers' attention focus (Gale & Schick, 2009).

Joint attention, a foundational component of communication, is the phenomenon during which at least two people share the same object of focus simultaneously. Parents and their children use joint attention to look at the same object, look at each other, or use alternating eye gaze, gestures, or words to direct each other's attention to something. Lammertink and colleagues (2021) found that joint attention skills had been linked to many communication skills, such as mutual gaze, looking at objects, and later vocabulary sizes. In their investigation, parents and their children were more likely to achieve more and longer moments of joint attention when they had congruence in hearing status; that is, when the parent and their child were both either hearing or deaf. However, they also discovered that hearing parents of deaf children were sensitive to their child's hearing status and often interacted with them differently than with hearing children, though they had shorter, less frequent moments of joint attention than deaf parents did.

Despite the relatively reduced joint attention between hearing parents and their deaf children, hearing parents do modify their approach to language and attention-getting with their children (Abu-Zhaya et al., 2019). For example, many hearing parents touch their child to signal the boundaries (beginning and end) of a spoken message, which may help their child to attend to the message better than they would otherwise. Hearing parents of deaf children tend to speak (orally) to their children as much as parents of hearing children do. Still, they often modify their utterances to match the deaf child's vocabulary size, length of time since amplification, and other factors. They also incorporate visual attention-getting strategies that parents of hearing children do not use as frequently. For deaf children who do not use listening devices, hearing parents use more multimodal attention-getting strategies such as tapping or placing items in the child's line of sight (Abu-Zhaya et al., 2019).

Children learn words faster when adults talk about the objects already holding the child's attention, rather than attempting to redirect the child's focus to something else (Tomasello & Farrar, 1986). When hearing infants focus on an object or event, parents can link the focus of the child's attention with language by speaking about it. Deaf mothers create a functionally equivalent link by employing a visual attention-following strategy, using space to introduce their signs in the same location as their child's attentional focus (Tomasello & Farrar, 1986). When they do so, the child sees both the focus of their attention and the language mapped onto it simultaneously and can benefit from the same joint attention advantage as a hearing child in a similar situation. This mirrors the reporting of Coppola and Senghas (forthcoming) on the development of direct and indirect deixis in Nicaraguan Sign Language (ISL, "Idioma de Señas de Nicaragua"); pointing began as a type of co-speech gesture but became linguistic over time. Further, newer research on the function of demonstratives in language acquisition suggests that signers exhibit different behaviors when joint attention is disrupted; specifically, facial expressions are used functionally as demonstratives to reestablish joint attention (Morford et al., 2019), and children have been shown to use gaze-shifting and shared gaze to maintain joint attention (Twitchell et al., 2022). Adult signers can use these strategies to map language onto the object of a child's attention.

"Parentese" and "motherese" describe the unique qualities of child-directed communication that exaggerate specific aspects of expression and elicit increased attention from young children. Speech-based parentese incorporates a greater variety of melodic contours, pitch ranges, rhythms, and repetition, with longer pauses and shorter utterances, than is typical for interactions with older children or adults (Fernald & Simon, 1984; Papoušek et al., 1987; Saint-Georges et al., 2013). Sign-based parentese incorporates clearer articulation, more frequent repetition, more exaggerated hand shapes and movements through space, and a slower tempo than adult-directed signing (Pizer et al., 2011). Pizer and colleagues (2011) described other parentese techniques employed by deaf parents including molding (overtly teaching a sign by manipulating the child's articulators to form it); signing on the child's body (sometimes alternated with signing on the parent's body, depending on positioning and context); displacement of a sign onto the object to which it referred or otherwise into the child's visual field; leaning into the child's visual field; and lengthening (slowing the movement or extending the final hold of a sign). Deaf infants pay greater attention and are more emotionally responsive to sign-based parentese than to adult-directed signing (Masataka, 1996, 1998). They also imitate signs more frequently in response to parentese (Pizer et al., 2011) than to adult-directed signing.

Touch also plays an important role in parent–child interactions and communication. Koester and colleagues (2000) described the phenomenon of infant-directed touch that may parallel the parentese in infant-directed speech and signing. They categorized the aspects of infant-directed touch by duration, threshold level (degree of sensitivity), number of parts of the body involved in touch, and intensity of touch. They found that deaf parents frequently used a "tap/sign" strategy, in which the parent tapped the infant's body, usually the arms or legs, to let them know that the parent was about to start signing. This strategy created joint attention by eliciting the infant's visual attention before signing (Loots & Devisé, 2003).

Hearing families can learn to use the intuitive communication techniques of deaf parents to hold their deaf children's attention, connect with them, and elicit greater language output by emulating the child-directed characteristics that deaf parents use (Koester & Lahti-Harper, 2010). In fact, some hearing mothers do intuitively compensate for their infant's reduced hearing levels by using highly animated facial expressions (Koester et al., 2000); however, the use of more high-level techniques would be even more helpful. Early intervention providers such as deaf mentors or teachers of the deaf can use the parent-coaching model to teach additional visual-tactile strategies to families and increase adult–child joint attention.

3.3.3 Techniques to Build Parental Self-Efficacy and Confidence

When their child is first identified as deaf, many families feel stressed or over-whelmed by the amount of information they must learn. When they begin early intervention services, they may also feel inept as a parent compared to the expertise of the early intervention providers (Roberts et al., 2016). Thus, interventions must focus on parent self-efficacy and empowerment in addition to the focus on the child's development (Wright et al., 2021). Self-efficacy is an individual's evaluation of their competence, confidence in their abilities, and perceived control in their ability to produce specific outcomes (Trivette et al., 2009). Parents' self-efficacy is positively related to their children's improvements in language skills over time (DesJardin, 2004; DesJardin & Eisenberg, 2007). Adult learning techniques that are effective for learning specific knowledge and skills do not necessarily also improve self-efficacy (Trivette et al., 2009), so it is valuable for providers to target self-efficacy as a distinct area of focus in their intervention and this is part of seeing the whole family as the unit of service provision (Sass-Lehrer et al., 2016).

When families were taught specific communicative and teaching strategies, Alper and colleagues (2020) found that although an increase in maternal self-efficacy was only marginally related to an increase in language strategy use, the lower mothers' use of strategies was at baseline, the greater the self-efficacy gains they demonstrated. Thus, families who do not yet use any language strategies with their children and are starting intervention with less background knowledge on improving their child's language may depend more on building a foundation of self-efficacy to begin using language strategies for the first time.

DesJardin and Eisenberg (2007) described the four primary sources of self-efficacy and linked them to the parents of deaf children with cochlear implants. Here, we extend that link to families of deaf children learning signed languages. The first source of parent self-efficacy is personal history. This history may include positive or negative experiences with parental responsibilities or with learning languages. A parent who has experienced raising a child, especially a deaf child, may feel more capable than a less-experienced parent as they face the familiar parts of the parenting journey (e.g., Rems-Smario, 2017b). As their child grows and they gain more and more experiences navigating the medical, educational, and social systems as a parent of a deaf child, their self-efficacy may also grow. Additionally, a parent who has successfully navigated a language-learning experience in the past may be more likely to persist through language-based struggles or frustrations as they learn to sign with their child.

The second source of self-efficacy is vicarious experience. A parent who has watched a close friend or family member navigate an experience similar to their own and succeed may feel more confident that they will also succeed in their journey. This can also apply to learning language skills and specific techniques they use with their child: The parent may gain confidence in the effectiveness of signed language by meeting other families with deaf children and learning about their experiences learning to sign and raising their children. This vicarious experience speaks to the importance of family-to-family support (DesJardin & Eisenberg, 2007; Gallegos et al., 2016). In 2018, the National Association of the Deaf (NAD) in the United States ran a campaign for families called "The Gift of Language" (NAD, 2022b). In it, they shared themed compilations of interviews with parents of deaf children. In the first video, called "Gift of Love," one parent mentioned how important a Parent Infant Program (PIP) was for her to interact with other parents (NADvlogs, 2018a); another shared, "[t]here's other people that have been through it" (NADvlogs, 2018b, 0:25–0:26). Unfortunately, many families report a lack of information from their medical and early intervention providers on how to find this type of support (Shezi & Joseph, 2021). Families gain invaluable vicarious experience by networking and sharing stories with fellow families of deaf children who have had the same experiences that they have. They are able to ask their questions in a safe space without feeling ignorant; learn to navigate the medical, educational, and social systems that they must navigate; and get honest, direct insight into providers, methods, and parenting decisions from other families who have "been there."

Another powerful source of vicarious experience for families includes deaf adults. Because most deaf adults were once deaf children, their retrospective insights on their childhood, education, and raising provide perspectives on growing up deaf that families may not have access to otherwise. Deaf adults can inform families about the decisions that their own families made when they were children, so that families who currently have young deaf children can use that information to inform their own decisions. Also, deaf adults provide aspirational capital – hopes and dreams for their child's future – by showing families, through their very existence, who their child could grow up to be (Crace et al., 2022; Pittman et al., 2016).

The third source of self-efficacy is verbal persuasion (DesJardin & Eisenberg, 2007). This describes becoming more confident in one's ability to handle life's challenges in response to verbal "pep talks" or feedback on an accomplishment. Providers can bolster families' self-efficacy by reassuring them regularly that they are doing a good job as a parent and are making progress in learning a signed language and language techniques. It is especially helpful to provide specific verbal feedback on what they are doing right, so families can feel confident in continuing to implement strategies during the majority of the time when the provider is not present. Providers can also help families identify who in their lives is a good source of verbal support. That way, families know who they can contact if they find their confidence faltering and have their self-efficacy renewed.

The fourth source of self-efficacy comes from emotional arousal and associated anticipation of failure or success (DesJardin & Eisenberg, 2007). If a person has a negative or unsuccessful experience, they often experience a high level of negative emotional arousal, or stress, when they think about that experience. That heightened stress can lead to feeling less efficacious about their ability to do well in a similar stressful situation. Conversely, a low level of emotional arousal is associated with higher self-efficacy because the individual feels less shaken up by the experience. Thus, if a parent has a stressful time with a particular provider, appointment, technique, or other parenting experience with their deaf child, they may lose confidence that they will be able to handle that situation effectively in the future. It is prudent for providers to be alert to families' stress levels and to remember the three other sources of self-efficacy. That way, if they notice that a parent is feeling stressed and inefficacious about a particular experience, the provider can recruit past history, vicarious experience, and verbal persuasion to bolster the parent's self-efficacy.

The more self-efficacious families feel, the more likely they are to implement what they have learned from providers. Maternal self-efficacy has been significantly linked to the frequency of use of several facilitative language techniques in mothers of children with cochlear implants, which was then positively linked to the children's receptive and expressive language skills (DesJardin & Eisenberg, 2007). Maternal self-efficacy has also been linked with a higher number of child-initiated conversational turns per minute, indicating that children whose families feel more confident about communicating with them are more likely to carry on long conversations with their families (Alper et al., 2021).

3.3.4 How Families Learn Language Techniques Effectively

Adults learn new skills in various ways. Dunst and Trivette (2009) synthesized four adult learning methods in a meta-analysis to determine which specific practices were effective for adult learning. They found that learners' active involvement in learning and judging their learning experience was related to stronger outcomes. The most effective processes for introducing new knowledge, material, or practices were out-of-class activities/self-instruction and warm-up exercises/pre-class quizzes. To illustrate the *use* of new knowledge, material, or practices, the most effective methods were role-playing/simulations and incorporating learner input to demonstrate how to apply the new information. Problem-solving, applying learned material to real-life situations, and playing learning games or doing writing exercises were also highly effective. When instructors engaged learners in determining their next steps for learning or had groups reflect on instructor or peer feedback, they were most effective in improving their performance. Comparing their performance to pre-established standards or criteria was effective for learners to assess their performance. Overall, the more adult learning characteristics were included in any given study in the meta-analysis, the larger the effect size was between those characteristics and the study outcome. Thus, the more evidence-based adult learning strategies are employed, the more the learners will learn and retain.

Some families use facilitative language techniques naturally, while others need direct instruction to learn them. Roberts and colleagues (2016) recommended applying the methods identified by Dunst and Trivette (2009) to teaching families to use language techniques with their children. These methods included introduction, illustration, practice, evaluation, reflection, and mastery. Dunst and Trivette (2009) further described the four-phase process of their Participatory Adult Learning Strategy (PALS) as starting with the trainer – the provider, in this case – introducing and illustrating the targeted knowledge or practice (e.g., a facilitative language technique), followed by the parent applying the technique themselves and evaluating the child's response. Then, the parent and the provider reflected on how it went, determined how the parent was progressing in mastering the technique, and then decided on the next steps. Active parental involvement at all stages was crucial for the success of this approach (Dunst & Trivette, 2009).

By drawing on the evidence base and clinical skills of SLPs and the visual and tactile expertise of deaf parents and signed language linguists, professionals who develop family-centered signed language curricula can create learning materials to teach families facilitative language techniques effectively. When they give families specific strategies for *using* their emerging signed language skills, providers can use a collaborative approach to support these families in creating an accessible, language-rich environment at home.

3.4 Deaf Community Cultural Wealth

Yosso described community cultural wealth as an "array of knowledge, skills, abilities, and contacts possessed and utilized by Communities of Color to survive and resist macro and micro-forms of oppression" (Yosso, 2005, p. 77). This lens highlighted how marginalized children's talents were often passed over for not conforming to expected norms (norms based on white, hearing children, mostly from upper-middle-class families). Deaf Community Cultural Wealth (DCCW) extended Yosso's work and directly applied it to deaf communities (Fleischer et al., 2015). It asserted that deaf people had their own types of cultural wealth that helped members of the deaf community "survive, if not thrive, in the dominant culture" (Braun et al., 2017, p. 16).

Teaching DCCW in a family-centered curriculum is important for two reasons: (1) Deaf children are predominantly born into hearing families (Mitchell & Karchmer, 2004), and (2) DCCW provides one way for hearing parents to develop self-efficacy in raising a deaf child, following the key ideas shared in Sections 3.3.3 and 3.3.4. In learning about DCCW, parents and families are empowered first to recognize the positive aspects of having a deaf person in their family, and second, to pass down this empowerment to their child, who will need these skills to navigate the predominantly hearing world.

In *ASL at Home*, DCCW is included in each chapter. The text invites readers to reflect on the concept of cultural wealth and a strengths-based approach – rather than a deficit one – to embark on an ASL and deaf-community learning journey with their young deaf child. Because DCCW is passed down from generation to generation (Fleischer et al., 2015), we want to help hearing families pass down this empowered mindset and skill set to their children and build a strong positive network for their children to develop holistically (Abrams & Gallegos, 2011; Lytle & Oliva, 2016).

3.5 The Case for Flexibility

Because families decide to learn a signed language at different stages in their journey of raising a deaf child, it is imperative that family-centered signed language curricula incorporate flexibility into their design and use. As described in Section 2.1.2, some families have access to classes, whether taught by a community organization, school/early intervention program, or other entity. These organizations can use a family-centered curriculum to tailor the learning experience to the family audience.

Additionally, many early intervention providers such as teachers of the deaf, deaf mentors, and/or SLPs use a parent-coaching approach in which they work directly with the parents and other family members to support the child's development. In that case, they can use a family-centered curriculum to teach signed language, language techniques, and DCCW during home visits or other services. The team can designate one provider to follow the curriculum during their visits while other providers serve the family differently, or the team can divide the curriculum. For example, the teacher of the deaf and the deaf mentor could divide up the signed language instruction and DCCW lessons, while the SLP addresses the facilitative language techniques. This approach allows each team member to take advantage of their strengths.

Finally, as described in Section 2.1, many families of deaf children note a severe lack of information on signed language acquisition in their hearing screening, identification, and early intervention experience. Even if they do not have access to classes or a supportive team of service providers, families who are self-driven to learn can use a family-centered signed language curriculum to learn independently. For this reason, a curriculum needs to include in-depth explanations in family-friendly language, accompanied by instructional videos with deaf language models, to facilitate families' independent learning processes. That way, they can learn at their own speed without depending on the service-provision system to give them what they need.

4 Feedback and Growth

After the book *ASL at Home* was released in late July 2020, families and service providers immediately started asking whether we would teach classes based on the curriculum. This was not something we had initially envisioned, but there seemed to be high demand for distance ASL learning (Crace et al., 2022). We decided to launch our first ASL class, *Learn ASL at Home*, in January 2021. By that time, we had already created a variety of supplemental materials for our curriculum, including vocabulary sheets (in both black and white and color versions, the latter complete with GIFs of signs) and flashcards (both printable and electronic), as well as a class kit including a Google Slides version of the curriculum to guide our class sessions. We taught the class on the Zoom teleconferencing platform.

4.1 Changes to Virtual Course Delivery

The first iteration of our course was five weeks long, with two-hour sessions each week. The first session was dedicated to class introductions – students took turns introducing themselves and explaining what brought them to the class – and a presentation about the class format and what the remaining four sessions would look like. Of the remaining four sessions, one was dedicated to each chapter in *ASL at Home*'s first edition, with roughly the first hour devoted to language instruction and the second hour devoted to explaining and practicing the language enrichment technique and discussing the Deaf Community Cultural Wealth lesson of the week.

After the first cohort, a student shared that it was sometimes difficult to follow the course with all the materials and emails back and forth sharing resources and announcements. She suggested it would be better to have a central place where all the materials were kept without the possibility of losing them in one's inbox. To address this, we introduced Google Classroom as a learning management system (LMS) for our second cohort, keeping everything else the same. We chose Google Classroom because it is ubiquitous and free. Also, many families learned to use it during the COVID-19 pandemic when many school districts used it for distance learning. It helps to streamline assignments and allows for better communication among the class community (Ventayen et al., 2018). Google Classroom is also helpful because of its mobile capabilities (Dash, 2019).

Using Google Classroom successfully addressed the students' challenges with keeping track of course materials and staying apprised of course communications. Now, before each new cohort starts, we provide a short written tutorial about Google Classroom organization and how to submit assignments to promote student learning and engagement (Octaberlina & Muslimin, 2020). During the first class session, we also provide a live tour of Google Classroom on Zoom.

The first two cohorts (the first without and the second with Google Classroom) followed the five-week, two-hour model. The first author served as the primary instructor and the second author served to teach the Deaf Community Cultural Wealth (DCCW) lesson and facilitate discussion about how it applied to the students' lives. The first author served as both the interpreter for the DCCW lesson and the instructor for other portions of the class. This was not ideal, as an interpreter should not also be participating in the interaction, and signed language instruction is best provided by deaf individuals; however, *ASL at Home* as an entity did not have funds for interpreting. Snoddon (2015) noted that early classes with parents were best taught by hearing instructors so students could have unimpeded access to the content. We encountered the dilemma that Snoddon described: How should access to the content be balanced with having deaf instructors? This weighed on us, and we discussed alternatives to this suboptimal arrangement.

After the second cohort, we received feedback that two hours represented a large time commitment for families of young children; they felt it was not family centered enough for this reason (Quiñonez Summer, 2022). In addition, one student commented on the five-week course, noting that they felt it was a waste of time to "build community" on the first day of such a short class. They believed it would be worth taking the time to get to know one another for a longer period, such as an eight-week class.

Considering these suggestions from an informal (and optional) feedback form after the class ended, and the issues surrounding access and interpreting, we decided to change the course format. The new (and current) course format is eight weeks long with one-hour sessions each time. Two weeks are devoted to each chapter with the split roughly mirroring that of the previous course model. Specifically, odd-numbered weeks are devoted to language instruction (roughly half for vocabulary instruction and half for expressive sentence practice) and even-numbered weeks are devoted to discussing DCCW and teaching the Language Enrichment Technique of the Week with sample scenarios. We have also been able to secure interpreting services through the second author's place of employment, which allows both instructors to participate freely and equitably, and for participants to have equitable access to both instructors. We also started recording class sessions and sharing class videos on Google Classroom with the understanding that only students may use them to review or catch up on a missed class.

As noted previously, parent-to-parent support is important for self-efficacy. It is also an important aspect of online learning (McElrath & McDowell, 2008), so we decided that it was important to build community in our class. To this end, students engage in a week of independent (asynchronous) work before beginning the eight weeks of synchronous sessions on Zoom. During this time, students complete several pre-class activities. These include two interactive slide presentations where students build a slide in a slide deck to (1) introduce themselves and their family and share what drew them to the course and (2) set and share their goals for the course. We also encourage students to view and comment on the slides their classmates create to get to know one another. This helps students know what they might learn from others. For example, if one family has an older child, they could share some expertise about how they navigated their child's earliest months and years with those families who have a child only several months old. Indeed, such a situation might serve to foster vicarious self-efficacy.

The other pre-class activities are to: read the introduction chapter of the textbook (Zarchy & Geer, 2020), view a mini-lecture via Google Slides, and share some reflections about the pre-class work in anticipation of the synchronous class sessions beginning the following week. The mini-lecture is an adapted version of the original presentation we used to share on day one of the five-week version of the class. Instead of a live presentation, short lecture videos are embedded into presentation slides, explaining what we would have explained had the session been live, following the general format described in Geer (2021). In "present" mode in Google Slides, users can click the embedded video – presented in ASL with English and Spanish subtitles – to view that portion of the presentation.

Another change we made to *Learn ASL at Home* classes based on feedback included moving instruction about fingerspelling out of the early chapters of the book. We continue to believe, and know that research supports (Allen, 2015; Padden, 1996), that it is never too early to expose young deaf children to fingerspelling. However, families reported that attempting to learn to fingerspell detracted from their ability to focus on other, more urgent aspects of the course, such as learning to interact with their children using multi-word utterances instead of single signs. To this end, we removed the fingerspelling lesson from the main lecture and moved it to its own slide presentation. In the mini-lecture, we briefly describe fingerspelling and share that a full lesson on fingerspelling is available for the learners to access whenever they feel ready, even though it is not a focus of the course.

Since changing to the eight-week format, we have taught seven cohorts, including one in Spanish, with positive comments on the format and pacing of the course. As *Learn ASL at Home* classes evolve, we consider new lesson formats that may be incorporated. Future iterations of our classes may include breakout rooms to practice engaging in conversations with one another (Gass & Mackey, 2015). This is also supported by the work of Dunst and Trivette (2009), who suggested that role-playing, problem-solving, and applying materials to real-life situations best support adult learning and material retention (refer back to Section 1.1.4 for more on this). Because the *ASL at Home* curriculum teaches infant- and child-directed language, we could set up a role-play activity where one participant plays the adult (e.g., parent, caretaker, etc.) and one plays the child (specifying the age or language ability of the child). We could provide prompts to push output, as Pannell and colleagues (2017) encourage as they translate the theory of the Output Hypothesis into practice.

4.2 Formal Survey on *ASL at Home*

In preparation for Zarchy and Geer (2022) and the present manuscript, we sent out a more formal survey (available in English and Spanish) using Qualtrics

Table 1 Ages of the survey respondents' children.

Age range	0;11	1–2;11	3–4;11	5–6;11	7–8;11	9–10;11
N	1	5	1	1	1	1
Total	10					

specifically for families who had used our curriculum and/or taken a class with us. [4] We submitted the protocol to the Institutional Review Board (IRB) for California State University, Sacramento, but were told that it did not constitute "human subjects research" and thus IRB approval was not required.

At the time of writing, twenty-three individuals had opened the survey, and twenty-two had consented to complete it. Nineteen respondents shared their relationship with a deaf child: ten were parents, one was a grandparent, four were professionals, and five had no relation to a deaf child. Because we had directed the survey only toward family members, data from (at most) eleven family members are described below, but there was some attrition as it was a rather long survey. Most questions had multiple choice, multiple answer, or Likert scale responses. Several optional open-ended questions asked for elaboration on Likert ratings and there was a final open-ended question at the end of the survey.

Table 1 presents the ages of the survey respondents' children. The focus of the *ASL at Home* curriculum is families with deaf children under five years of age, but courses can be modified for older children as needed (for example, we once taught the parent of a nine year old and the step-parent of a twelve year old).

Of these ten respondents, on a question where they could select more than one answer, five indicated that they used the curriculum on their own, three took a class, one used the curriculum with a service provider, and two indicated "none of these." Before using *ASL at Home*, five respondents said they had no ASL proficiency, and three indicated they could form basic sentences including asking and answering simple questions.

After using the curriculum, four respondents (everyone who answered this question) indicated feeling more confident in signing with their child. Three strongly agreed that they used ASL more with their child since using *ASL at Home*. In elaboration on this question, one respondent noted that they "felt a greater sense of competence and a greater willingness to identify additional resources to help [them] learn the language."

---

[4] Some service providers have also taken *Learn ASL at Home* classes with us, but for the purposes of this project, we focused only on information collected from family members of deaf and hard-of-hearing children.

Respondents were satisfied with the number of vocabulary words taught per chapter, though several wished there were more. Most respondents strongly agreed that the vocabulary was useful and easy to apply to daily routines and that the expressive and receptive language practice activities were helpful. Most also agreed or strongly agreed that language enrichment techniques and fridge posters (for families to post on their refrigerator as a reminder of the "technique of the week") were helpful and helped them to feel more comfortable using language techniques.

Most agreed or strongly agreed that the DCCW discussions helped them understand the importance of having a connection with their deaf child and it helped them understand the benefits of bi- or multilingualism. They felt more confident about seeking out deaf community resources for their child, and the DCCW lessons helped them feel more positive about their child's future.

All respondents agreed or strongly agreed that the ASL lessons, language enrichment techniques, and DCCW offered practical applications to their lives. At the end of the survey, we asked, "What else would you like us to know about your experience using this curriculum?" We received four responses:

- "I think it is an excellent class to take when a parent first finds out their child is deaf/hard of hearing; I really liked it but would have used the concepts more if I had taken it when my child was younger."
- "It was amazing. I wish more families [could] maintain consistent attendance."
- "Would love more modules, as this barely scratches the surface!"
- "I eagerly anticipate participating again when additional material has been prepared."

More formal assessments of this curriculum, including semi-structured interviews or a more structured group experiment to compare another curriculum or no curriculum with *ASL at Home*, would be informative. However, according to these preliminary data, *ASL at Home* appears helpful for families. While it would be difficult to do a fully randomized controlled trial because there is an extent to which groups are self-selecting – certain people sign up for certain types of classes while others may sign up for something different – more formalized assessment of curriculum efficacy is necessary in the future. Future surveys should be shorter to avoid participant attrition across questions and could be combined with other qualitative and quantitative data. To the extent appropriate for this program, it may be helpful to start with a close replication of Oyserman and de Geus (2021).

4.2.1 ASL at Home's *Second Edition*

The second edition of our book (Zarchy & Geer, 2023) provides the additional modules that a survey respondent requested in their comment shared in Section 4.2. The new book has eight chapters in addition to the original four. All twelve chapters are centered around daily routines. As we prepared the second edition, we conducted an informal poll on social media asking followers which routines would be most helpful to them and then selected the eight that were most frequently suggested. Like the original four chapters, each new chapter has a short vocabulary list, language instruction lessons, language enrichment techniques of increasing difficulty, and DCCW that takes a deeper dive as the book continues. While the book was not designed specifically to align with CEFR (Council of Europe, 2022b), the new curriculum addresses the skills listed in Table 2.

4.2.2 *Future Modifications to* Learn ASL at Home *Courses*

The more we teach the *Learn ASL at Home* course, the more we reflect on what works and what we could do better. In preparing for this project, we found an article about adult learners (Dunst & Trivette, 2009) which helped to solidify some of the ideas we were already considering. For example, Dunst and Trivette (2009) found that learning is most effective when students have opportunities to practice a new skill, evaluate the consequences of applying that skill, and then reflect on and assess their acquisition of the new knowledge. To this end, we implement graded quizzes in our most recent cohort (rather than credit/no credit) to raise the stakes. Reflections assignments at the conclusion of each chapter were required rather than optional. In upcoming cohorts, we will also create a quiz to assess the completion of the pre-class asynchronous activities noted in the previous subsection. This will help ensure that everyone is on the same page and ready to engage fully with the learning process when they enter the course. Finally, we will incorporate breakout rooms for learners to get more input, output, and interaction practice (Gass & Mackey, 2015) through role-play activities.

After the publication of the second edition of the curriculum, we will create two new *Learn ASL at Home* classes. The currently available class will be renamed *Learn ASL at Home: Chapters 1–4*. The new classes will be *Learn ASL at Home: Chapters 5–8* and *Learn ASL at Home: Chapters 9–12*. The two new classes will follow the same format as the first, starting with a week of pre-class activities to be done independently (including review quizzes of previously covered material) and community-building activities. Next, there will be eight weeks of instruction following the same format of odd-numbered weeks devoted to language instruction and even-numbered weeks devoted to DCCW

Table 2 CEFR skills taught in the forthcoming *ASL at Home, Second Edition* (Zarchy & Geer, 2023), modified from (Council of Europe, 2022a).

Basic user	Expressive skills	Receptive skills
A2	Can *describe* in simple terms areas of immediate need	Can *understand* sentences and frequently used expressions related to areas of most immediate relevance
	Can *communicate* in simple and routine tasks requiring a simple and direct exchange of information on familiar and routine matters	
A1	Can *produce* sentences and frequently used expressions related to areas of most immediate relevance	
	Can *produce* very basic phrases aimed at the satisfaction of needs of a concrete type	Can *understand* very basic phrases aimed at the satisfaction of needs of a concrete type
	Can *interact* in a simple way provided the other person signs slowly and clearly	

and language enrichment techniques. In keeping with family-centered principles (Quiñonez Summer, 2022), we do not want a class longer than eight weeks (cf. Snoddon, 2015), as the first author has experienced a significant drop-off in the classes he teaches for his school district at the eight-week mark. Thus, we will keep the same structure of eight-week classes covering four chapters each, rather than all twelve chapters being covered in a single class.

Just as families of deaf children continue to learn and grow with their children, our family-centered curriculum and its associated classes and learning materials will continue to grow as we learn more about what families need to create a language-rich home where their deaf child can flourish.

5 Conclusion

"Parents are children's first teachers" (NAD, 2022a, para. 1). Hearing families of deaf children urgently need to learn a signed language so they can provide an accessible home environment where their children can acquire language and reach their full potential. We propose developing family-centered curricula for signed languages worldwide, based on research into adult second language learning, child first language acquisition, evidence-based facilitative language techniques, the unique needs of families, and Deaf Community Cultural Wealth. These curricula will have the greatest impact when they are embedded in the daily routines of young children and are designed to be provided flexibly in a variety of formats and settings. These curricula can be developed following accepted standards and guidelines for second language learning like ACTFL and CEFR (refer back to Table 2 for a description of how the forthcoming second edition of *ASL at Home* aligns with CEFR). The more family-centered learning opportunities are made available, the more deaf children may evade language deprivation.

Appendix

*How to Create a Family-Centered Curriculum:
A Tutorial*

Choose common daily routines in the lives of young children	• Choose linked sequences of activities that are repeated every day – or nearly every day – with some consistent elements, even when there is variation. • Examples: meal time; bath time; diaper change and bathroom routines; book sharing; bedtime; playtime; arts, crafts, and sensory activities; outdoors; cleaning up; getting dressed; family time; and pets.
Determine frequently used core vocabulary related to each routine	• Core vocabulary includes words from a variety of word classes, such as pronouns, verbs, adjectives, adverbs, prepositions, determiners, conjunctions, interjections, question words, and nouns. • Keep the number of words low in each lesson to avoid overwhelm.
Develop simple sentences containing the core vocabulary, building cumulatively	• Expressive sentence-based activities provide families with "hands-up" practice opportunities, facilitating increased motor coordination in the new modality, and encouraging them to sign with each other throughout their day. Teach grammar as it becomes necessary to use in daily routines. • Receptive sentence-based activities provide opportunities to understand whole sentences, even if their child is not yet signing at that level, to prepare them for when their child begins to produce signed language of increasing length and complexity. These activities are also useful formative assessments to gauge progress.
Teach evidence-based facilitative language techniques in family-friendly language	• These lessons allow curriculum developers to collaborate with speech-language pathologists (SLPs), teachers of the deaf (ToDs), or other similar professionals. • Begin at a simple level and increase in difficulty as families gain experience using techniques.

(cont.)

Incorporate Deaf Community Cultural Wealth lessons	• These lessons are discussion based and can include thought questions about any and all types of cultural capital: familial capital; linguistic capital; social capital; aspirational capital; navigational capital; resistant capital.
	• Two approaches:
	  ○ Teach the concept of cultural wealth by stimulating introspection about their own cultural wealth.
	  ○ Direct instruction on deaf culture and community resources.

Make the curriculum available to service providers and families	• Make your tools available to early intervention providers, families, and other stakeholders so the largest possible number of families can benefit from your resources.

References

Abrams, S. (Director). (2014, April 7). An overview of the deaf mentor program at New Mexico School for the Deaf [Video]. YouTube. https://youtu.be/snE4pD882v4.

Abrams, S., & Gallegos, R. (2011). Making a critical difference in New Mexico. *Odyssey*, *12*, 24–27. https://eric.ed.gov/?id=EJ945005.

Abu-Zhaya, R., Kondaurova, M. V., Houston, D., & Seidl, A. (2019). Vocal and tactile input to children who are deaf or hard of hearing. *Journal of Speech, Language, and Hearing Research*, *62*(7), 2372–2385. https://doi.org/10.1044/2019_JSLHR-L-18-0185.

Allen, T. E. (2015). ASL skills, fingerspelling ability, home communication context and early alphabetic knowledge of preschool-aged deaf children. *Sign Language Studies*, *15*(3), 233–265. https://doi.org/10.1353/sls.2015.0006.

Alper, R. M., Beiting, M., Luo, R. et al. (2021). Change the things you can: Modifiable parent characteristics predict high-quality early language interaction within socioeconomic status. *Journal of Speech, Language, and Hearing Research*, *64*(6), 1992–2004. https://doi.org/10.1044/2021_JSLHR-20-00412.

Alper, R. M., Hurtig, R. R., & McGregor, K. K. (2020). The role of maternal psychosocial perceptions in parent-training programs: A preliminary randomized controlled trial. *Journal of Child Language*, *47*(2), 358–381. https://doi.org/10.1017/S0305000919000138.

Ambrose, S. E., Walker, E. A., Unflat-Berry, L. M., Oleson, J. J., & Moeller, M. P. (2015). Quantity and quality of caregivers' linguistic input to 18-month and 3-year-old children who are hard of hearing. *Ear and Hearing*, *36*, 48S–59S. https://doi.org/10.1097/AUD.0000000000000209.

American Council on the Teaching of Foreign Languages (ACTFL). (2012). ACTFL Proficiency Guidelines 2012. www.actfl.org/resources/actfl-proficiency-guidelines-2012.

American Society for Deaf Children. (2022). https://deafchildren.org/.

Asmal, A., & Kaneko, M. (2020). Visual vernacular in South African Sign Language. *Sign Language Studies*, *20*(3), 491–517. https://doi.org/10.1353/sls.2020.0010.

Aurélio, F. S., & Tochetto, T. M. (2010). Triagem auditiva neonatal: Experiências de diferentes países. *Arquivos Internacionais de Otorrinolaringologia (Impresso)*, *14*(3), 355–363. https://doi.org/10.1590/S1809-48722010000300014.

Baker-Shenk, C., & Cokely, D. (1991). *American Sign Language green books, a teacher's resource text on grammar and culture.* Gallaudet University Press.

Banajee, M., Dicarlo, C., & Buras Stricklin, S. (2003). Core vocabulary determination for toddlers. *Augmentative and Alternative Communication, 19*(2), 67–73. https://doi.org/10.1080/0743461031000112034.

Barber, A. B., Swineford, L., Cook, C., & Belew, A. (2020). Effects of Project ImPACT parent-mediated intervention on the spoken language of young children with Autism Spectrum Disorder. *Perspectives of the ASHA Special Interest Groups, 5*(3), 573–581. https://doi.org/10.1044/2020_PERSP-20-10005.

Benedict, R., & Stecker, E. (2011). Early intervention: The missing link. *Journal of American Sign Languages and Literatures.* https://journalofasl.com/ei/.

Blackwell, A. K. M., Harding, S., Babayiğit, S., & Roulstone, S. (2015). Characteristics of parent–child interactions: A systematic review of studies comparing children with primary language impairment and their typically developing peers. *Communication Disorders Quarterly, 36*(2), 67–78. https://doi.org/10.1177/1525740114540202.

Blanco, C. (2020, February 27). Goldilocks and the CEFR levels: Which proficiency level is just right? *Duolingo Blog.* https://blog.duolingo.com/goldilocks-and-the-cefr-levels-which-proficiency-level-is-just-right/.

Boenisch, J., & Soto, G. (2015). The oral core vocabulary of typically developing English-speaking school-aged children: Implications for AAC practice. *Augmentative and Alternative Communication, 31*(1), 77–84. https://doi.org/10.3109/07434618.2014.1001521.

Boyce, L. K., Gillam, S. L., Innocenti, M. S., Cook, G. A., & Ortiz, E. (2013). An examination of language input and vocabulary development of young Latino dual language learners living in poverty. *First Language, 33*(6), 572–593. https://doi.org/10.1177/0142723713503145.

Braun, D. C., Gormally, C., & Clark, M. D. (2017). The deaf mentoring survey: A community cultural wealth framework for measuring mentoring effectiveness with underrepresented students. *CBE – Life Sciences Education, 16*(1), ar10. https://doi.org/10.1187/cbe.15-07-0155.

Brick, K. (2019, August 8). Deaf ecosystem in science [Conference Presentation]. DEAF-ROC (Deaf Engaged Academic Forum) Conference, Rochester, NY. https://rochester.hosted.panopto.com/Panopto/Pages/Viewer.aspx?id=11d5a4d7-d81d-449a-a1b9-aaa301356e37.

Brock, A. S., & Bass-Ringdahl, S. M. (2021). Facilitative language techniques used in the home by caregivers of young children who are deaf or hard of hearing. *Perspectives of the ASHA Special Interest Groups*, *6*(5), 1137–1145. https://doi.org/10.1044/2021_PERSP-20-00297.

Brooks, R., Singleton, J. L., & Meltzoff, A. N. (2020). Enhanced gaze-following behavior in Deaf infants of Deaf parents. *Developmental Science*, *23*(2), 1–10. https://doi.org/10.1111/desc.12900.

Brown, R. (2013). *A first language: The early stages*. Harvard University Press.

Buschmann, A., Jooss, B., Rupp, A. et al. (2008). Parent based language intervention for 2-year-old children with specific expressive language delay: A randomised controlled trial. *Archives of Disease in Childhood*, *94* (2), 110–116. https://doi.org/10.1136/adc.2008.141572.

Callanan, J., Ronan, K. R., & Signal, T. (2021). *Activating parents in early intervention: The role of relationship in functional and family gains. Treatment manual – Parent Child Relationally Informed Early Intervention.* The Informed SLP.

Callanan, J., Signal, T., & McAdie, T. (2021). Involving parents in early intervention: Therapists' experience of the Parent-Child Relationally Informed-Early Intervention (PCRI-EI) model of practice. *International Journal of Disability, Development and Education*, *70*, 1–14. https://doi.org/10.1080/1034912X.2021.1910933.

Caselli, N. K., Pyers, J., & Lieberman, A. M. (2021). Deaf children of hearing parents have age-level vocabulary growth when exposed to American Sign Language by 6 months of age. *The Journal of Pediatrics*, *70*(5), 674–687. https://doi.org/10.1016/j.jpeds.2021.01.029.

Cassell, J., & Cox, D. (1996). *Bravo ASL! curriculum* (K. Holland & D. Cox, Eds.). Amer Sign Language Productions.

Centers for Disease Control and Prevention (CDC). (2015). Early Hearing Detection and Intervention (EHDI) in Latin America. www.cdc.gov/ncbddd/hearingloss/ehdi-latin.html.

Chen Pichler, D. (2009). Sign production by first-time hearing signers: A closer look at handshape accuracy. *Cadernos de Saúde*, *2* (Número especial de Línguas Gestuais), 37–50.

Chen Pichler, D. (2021). Constructing a profile of successful L2 signer hearing parents of deaf children. National Museum of Ethnology. https://doi.org/10.15021/00009871.

Chen Pichler, D., Gale, E., & Lillo-Martin, D. (2021). Stuck at beginner level: Hearing parents' challenges in learning ASL word order. Early Hearing Detection and Intervention Annual Conference, Online, March 2–5, 2021. https://ehdiconference.org/archive/2021/index.cfm.

Cheng, Q., Halgren, E., & Mayberry, R. I. (2018). Effects of early language deprivation: Mapping between brain and behavioral outcomes. In

Proceedings of the 42nd Annual Boston University Conference on Language Development (pp. 140–152). Cascadilla Press.

Cheng, Q., Roth, A., Halgren, E., & Mayberry, R. I. (2019). Effects of early language deprivation on brain connectivity: Language pathways in deaf native and late first-language learners of American Sign Language. *Frontiers in Human Neuroscience, 13*, 1–12. https://doi.org/10.3389/fnhum.2019.00320.

Ching, T. Y. C., Dillon, H., Button, L. et al. (2017). Age at intervention for permanent hearing loss and 5-year language outcomes. *Pediatrics, 140*(3), 1–11. https://doi.org/10.1542/peds.2016-4274.

Clark, M. D., Cue, K. R., Delgado, N. J., Greene-Woods, A. N., & Wolsey, J.-L. A. (2020). Early intervention protocols: Proposing a default bimodal bilingual approach for deaf children. *Maternal and Child Health Journal, 24*(11), 1339–1344. https://doi.org/10.1007/s10995-020-03005-2.

Cleave, P. L., Becker, S. D., Curran, M. K., Van Horne, A. J. O., & Fey, M. E. (2015). The efficacy of recasts in language intervention: A systematic review and meta-analysis. *American Journal of Speech-Language Pathology, 24*(2), 237–255. https://doi.org/10.1044/2015_AJSLP-14-0105.

Coker, C. A. (2022). *Motor learning and control for practitioners* (Fifth Edition). Routledge.

Cook, P. S. (2011). Features in American Sign Language storytelling. *Storytelling, Self, Society, 7*(1), 36–62. https://doi.org/10.1080/15505340.2011.535723.

Costa, E. A., Day, L., Caverly, C. et al. (2019). Parent-Child Interaction Therapy as a behavior and spoken language intervention for young children with hearing loss. *Language, Speech, and Hearing Services in Schools, 50*, 34–52. https://doi.org/10.1044/2018_LSHSS-18-0054.

Council of Europe. (2022a). Global scale – Table 1 (CEFR 3.3): Common reference levels. www.coe.int/en/web/common-european-framework-reference-languages/table-1-cefr-3.3-common-reference-levels-global-scale.

Council of Europe. (2022b). The CEFR levels. www.coe.int/en/web/common-european-framework-reference-languages/level-descriptions.

Crace, J., Rems-Smario, J., & Nathanson, G. (2022). Deaf professionals and community involvement with early education. In L. R. Schmeltz (Ed.), *The NCHAM eBook: A resource guide for Early Hearing Detection and Intervention (EHDI)* (pp. 1–14). National Center for Hearing Assessment and Management, Utah State University.

Curtiss, S., Fromkin, V., Krashen, S., Rigler, D., & Rigler, M. (1974). The linguistic development of Genie. *Language, 50*(3), 528–554. https://doi.org/10.2307/412222.

Dash, S. (2019). Google Classroom as a learning management system to teach biochemistry in a medical school. *Biochemistry and Molecular Biology Education, 47*(4), 404–407. https://doi.org/10.1002/bmb.21246.

Davidson, K., Lillo-Martin, D., & Chen Pichler, D. (2014). Spoken English language development among native signing children with cochlear implants. *Journal of Deaf Studies and Deaf Education, 19*(2), 238–250. https://doi.org/10.1093/deafed/ent045.

Davidson, L. S., Osman, A., & Geers, A. E. (2021). The effects of early intervention on language growth after age 3 for children with permanent hearing loss. *Journal of Early Hearing Detection and Intervention, 6*(1), 1–11. https://doi.org/10.26077/aa92-7cb7.

De Meulder, M. (2019). "So, why do you sign?" Deaf and hearing new signers, their motivation, and revitalisation policies for sign languages. *Applied Linguistics Review, 10*(4), 705–724. https://doi.org/10.1515/applirev-2017-0100.

Decker, K. B., & Vallotton, C. D. (2016). Early intervention for children with hearing loss: Information parents receive about supporting children's language. *Journal of Early Intervention, 38*(3), 151–169. https://doi.org/10.1177/1053815116653448.

DeKeyser, R. (2015). Skill acquisition theory. In B. VanPatten & J. Williams (Eds.), *Theories in second language acquisition: An introduction* (2nd ed., pp. 94–112). Routledge.

DesJardin, J. L. (2004). *Maternal self-efficacy and involvement: Supporting language development in young deaf children with cochlear implants* [Doctoral dissertation]. California State University, Los Angeles – University of California, Los Angeles.

DesJardin, J. L. (2006). Family empowerment: Supporting language development in young children who are deaf or hard of hearing. *The Volta Review, 106*(3), 275–298. https://doi.org/10.17955/tvr.106.3.m.574.

DesJardin, J. L., & Eisenberg, L. S. (2007). Maternal contributions: Supporting language development in young children with cochlear implants. *Ear & Hearing, 28*(4), 456–469. https://doi.org/10.1097/AUD.0b013e31806dc1ab.

Duchesne, L., & Marschark, M. (2019). Effects of age at cochlear implantation on vocabulary and grammar: A review of the evidence. *American Journal of Speech-Language Pathology, 28*(4), 1673–1691. https://doi.org/10.1044/2019_AJSLP-18-0161.

Dunst, C. J., & Trivette, C. M. (2009). Let's be PALS: An evidence-based approach to professional development. *Infants & Young Children, 22*(3), 164–176. https://doi.org/10.1097/IYC.0b013e3181abe169.

Dutra, N. J. (2020). *Including the deaf child at the dinner table: When and why hearing parents learn sign language* [Ed.D. dissertation]. California State University, Sacramento.

Elliott, K., Vears, D. F., Sung, V., Poulakis, Z., & Sheehan, J. (2022). Exploring parent support needs during the newborn hearing diagnosis pathway. *Journal of Clinical Medicine, 11*(5), 1389. https://doi.org/10.3390/jcm11051389.

Enns, C., & Price, L. (2013, June). Family involvement in ASL acquisition. *Visual Language & Visual Learning (VL2) Learning from Science: Research Brief, Research Brief #9.* https://vl2.gallaudet.edu/research-briefs/265.

Fant, L. (1994). *The American Sign Language phrase book by Lou Fant.* Contemporary Books.

Ferjan Ramírez, N., Lytle, S. R., & Kuhl, P. K. (2020). Parent coaching increases conversational turns and advances infant language development. *Proceedings of the National Academy of Sciences, 117*(7), 3484–3491. https://doi.org/10.1073/pnas.1921653117.

Fernald, A., & Simon, T. (1984). Expanded intonation contours in mothers' speech to newborns. *Developmental Psychology, 20*(1), 104–113.

Finocchiaro, M., & Brumfit, C. (1983). *The functional-notional approach: From theory to practice.* Oxford University Press.

Fleischer, F., Garrow, W., & Friedman-Narr, R. (2015). Developing deaf education. In W. W. Murawski & K. L. Scott (Eds.), *What really works in secondary education.* Corwin, a SAGE company. https://sk.sagepub.com/books/what-really-works-in-secondary-education.

Gale, E., Berke, M., Benedict, B., Olson, S., Putz, K., & Yoshinaga-Itano, C. (2021). Deaf adults in early intervention programs. *Deafness & Education International, 23*(1), 3–24. https://doi.org/10.1080/14643154.2019.1664795.

Gale, E., & Schick, B. (2009). Symbol-infused joint attention and language use in mothers with deaf and hearing toddlers. *American Annals of the Deaf, 153*(5), 484–503. https://doi.org/10.1353/aad.0.0066.

Gallegos, R., Halus, K., & Crace, J. (2016). Individualized family service plans and programming. In M. Sass-Lehrer (Ed.), *Early intervention for deaf and hard-of-hearing infants, toddlers, and their families: Interdisciplinary perspectives* (pp. 135–166). Oxford University Press.

Gárate, M., & Lenihan, S. (2016). Collaboration for communication, language, and cognitive development. In M. Sass-Lehrer (Ed.), *Early intervention for deaf and hard-of-hearing infants, toddlers, and their families: Interdisciplinary perspectives* (pp. 233–273). Oxford University Press.

Gass, S. M., & Mackey, A. (2015). Input, interaction, and output in second language acquisition. In B. VanPatten & J. Williams (Eds.), *Theories in second language acquisition: An introduction* (2nd ed., pp. 180–206) Routledge.

Geer, L. C. (2021). All in with Google Slides: Virtual engagement and formative assessment in introductory sign language linguistics. *Proceedings of the Linguistic Society of America, 6*(2), 5103. https://doi.org/10.3765/plsa.v6i2.5103.

Girolametto, L., Pearce, P. S., & Weitzman, E. (1996). Interactive focused stimulation for toddlers with expressive vocabulary delays. *Journal of Speech, Language, and Hearing Research, 39*(6), 1274–1283. https://doi .org/10.1044/jshr.3906.1274.

Girolametto, L., Pearce, P. S., & Weitzman, E. (2016). The effects of focused stimulation for promoting vocabulary in young children with delays: A pilot study. *Journal of Children's Communication Development.* https://doi.org/ 10.1177/152574019501700205.

Glickman, N. S., Crump, C., & Hamerdinger, S. (2020). Language deprivation is a game changer for the clinical specialty of deaf mental health. *Journal of the American Deafness and Rehabilitation Association, 54*(1), 54–89. https:// nsuworks.nova.edu/jadara/vol54/iss1/4.

Glickman, N. S., & Hall, W. C. (2018). Language deprivation and deaf mental health. In N. S. Glickman & W. C. Hall (Eds.), *Language deprivation and deaf mental health* (1st ed., pp. 24–53). Routledge. https://doi.org/10.4324/ 9781315166728-2.

Goldin-Meadow, S. (1982). The resilience of recursion: A study of a communication system developed without a conventional language model. In E. Wanner & L. R. Gleitman (Eds.), *Language acquisition: The state of the art* (pp. 51–77). Norton.

Goodwin, C., Carrigan, E., Walker, K., & Coppola, M. (2022). Language not auditory experience is related to parent-reported executive functioning in preschool-aged deaf and hard-of-hearing children. *Child Development, 93* (1), 209–224. https://doi.org/10.1111/cdev.13677.

Goodwin, C., Prunier, L., & Lillo-Martin, D. (2019). Parental sign input to Deaf children of Deaf parents: Vocabulary and syntax. In M. M. Brown & B. Dailey (Eds.), *Proceedings of the 43rd Boston University Conference on Language Development* (pp. 286–297). Cascadilla Press.

Haile, L. M., Kamenov, K., Briant, P. S. et al. (2021). Hearing loss prevalence and years lived with disability, 1990–2019: Findings from the Global Burden of Disease Study 2019. *The Lancet, 397*(10278), 996–1009. https://doi.org/ 10.1016/S0140-6736(21)00516-X.

Hall, M. L. (2020). The input matters: Assessing cumulative language access in deaf and hard of hearing individuals and populations. *Frontiers in Psychology, 11*, 1407. https://doi.org/10.3389/fpsyg.2020.01407.

Hall, M. L., Eigsti, I.-M., Bortfeld, H., & Lillo-Martin, D. (2017). Auditory deprivation does not impair executive function, but language deprivation might: Evidence from a parent-report measure in deaf native signing children. *Journal of Deaf Studies and Deaf Education, 22*(1), 9–21. https://doi.org/10.1093/deafed/enw054.

Hall, M. L., Eigsti, I.-M., Bortfeld, H., & Lillo-Martin, D. (2018). Executive function in deaf children: Auditory access and language access. *Journal of Speech, Language, and Hearing Research, 61*(8), 1970–1988. https://doi.org/10.1044/2018_JSLHR-L-17-0281.

Hall, W. C. (2017). What you don't know can hurt you: The risk of language deprivation by impairing sign language development in deaf children. *Maternal and Child Health Journal, 21*(5), 961–965. https://doi.org/10.1007/s10995-017-2287-y.

Hall, W. C., Levin, L. L., & Anderson, M. L. (2017). Language deprivation syndrome: A possible neurodevelopmental disorder with sociocultural origins. *Social Psychiatry and Psychiatric Epidemiology, 52*(6), 761–776. https://doi.org/10.1007/s00127-017-1351-7.

Hamilton, B., & Clark, M. D. M. (2020). The deaf mentor program: Benefits to families. *Psychology, 11*(5), 713–736. https://doi.org/10.4236/psych.2020.115049.

Harris, M., & Mohay, H. (1997). Learning to look in the right place: A comparison of attentional behavior in deaf children with deaf and hearing mothers. *Journal of Deaf Studies and Deaf Education, 2*(2), 95–103. https://doi.org/10.1093/oxfordjournals.deafed.a014316.

Hassanzadeh, S. (2012). Outcomes of cochlear implantation in deaf children of deaf parents: Comparative study. *The Journal of Laryngology & Otology, 126* (10), 989–994. https://doi.org/10.1017/S0022215112001909.

Henner, J., Caldwell-Harris, C. L., Novogrodsky, R., & Hoffmeister, R. (2016). American Sign Language syntax and analogical reasoning skills are influenced by early acquisition and age of entry to signing schools for the deaf. *Frontiers in Psychology, 7*, 1982. https://doi.org/10.3389/fpsyg.2016.01982.

Hintermair, M. (2006). Parental resources, parental stress, and socioemotional development of deaf and hard of hearing children. *Journal of Deaf Studies and Deaf Education, 11*(4), 493–513. https://doi.org/10.1093/deafed/enl005.

Hintermair, M. (2016). Foreword. In M. Sass-Lehrer (Ed.), *Early intervention for deaf and hard-of-hearing infants, toddlers, and their families: Interdisciplinary perspectives* (pp. ix–xiv). Oxford University Press.

Hopper, M. J. (2011). *Positioned as bystanders: Deaf students' experiences and perceptions of informal learning phenomena* [Ph.D. dissertation]. University of Rochester. https://urresearch.rochester.edu/fileDownloadForInstitutionalItem.action;jsessionid=6FE6002A04E5F7E082A5F478828AD4B8?itemId=14524&itemFileId=33679.

Humphries, T., Kushalnagar, P., Mathur, G. et al. (2016). Language choices for deaf infants: Advice for parents regarding sign languages. *Clinical Pediatrics*, *55*(6), 513–517. https://doi.org/10.1177/0009922815616891.

Humphries, T., & Padden, C. A. (2004). *Learning American Sign Language: Levels I & II – Beginning & Intermediate* (2nd ed.). Pearson Education, Inc.

Individuals with Disabilities Education Act, no. 33 (2004). https://sites.ed.gov/idea/statute-chapter-33/.

Johnson, S., Stapleton, L., & Berrett, B. (2020). Deaf Community Cultural Wealth in community college students. *The Journal of Deaf Studies and Deaf Education*, *25*(4), 438–446. https://doi.org/10.1093/deafed/enaa016.

Joint Committee on Infant Hearing. (2019). Year 2019 position statement: Principles and guidelines for early hearing detection and intervention programs. *Journal of Early Hearing Detection and Intervention*, *4*(2), 1–44. https://doi.org/10.15142/FPTK-B748.

Kaipa, R., & Danser, M. L. (2016). Efficacy of auditory-verbal therapy in children with hearing impairment: A systematic review from 1993 to 2015. *International Journal of Pediatric Otorhinolaryngology*, *86*, 124–134. https://doi.org/10.1016/j.ijporl.2016.04.033.

Kaiser, A. P., & Hancock, T. B. (2003). Teaching parents new skills to support their young children's development. *Infants & Young Children*, *16*(1), 9–21.

Kemp, P., & Turnbull, A. P. (2014). Coaching with parents in early intervention: An interdisciplinary research synthesis. *Infants & Young Children*, *27*(4), 305–324. https://doi.org/10.1097/IYC.0000000000000018.

Kestner, K. (2021). *Hausegebärdensprachkurs für hörgeschägigte Kinder (Home sign langauge course for hearing impaired children)*. https://web.kestner.de/shop/lernen-lehren/hausgebaerdensprachkurs-fuer-hoergeschaedigte-kinder/.

Koester, L. S., Brooks, L., & Traci. (2000). Tactile contact by deaf and hearing mothers during face-to-face interactions with their infants. *Journal of Deaf Studies and Deaf Education*, *5*(2), 127–139. https://doi.org/10.1093/deafed/5.2.127.

Koester, L. S., & Lahti-Harper, E. (2010). Mother-infant hearing status and intuitive parenting behaviors during the first 18 months. *American Annals of the Deaf*, *155*(1), 5–18. https://doi.org/10.1353/aad.0.0134.

Korver, A. M. H., Smith, R. J. H., Van Camp, G. et al. (2017). Congenital hearing loss. *Nature Reviews. Disease Primers*, *3*, 16094. https://doi.org/10.1038/nrdp.2016.94.

Lammertink, I., Hermans, D., Stevens, A. et al. (2021). Joint attention in the context of hearing loss: A meta-analysis and narrative synthesis. *The Journal of Deaf Studies and Deaf Education*, *27*(1), 1–15. https://doi.org/10.1093/deafed/enab029.

Lane, H. L., Hoffmeister, R., & Bahan, B. J. (1996). *A journey into the Deafworld* (pp. x, 513). Dawn Sign Press.

Lentz, E. M., Mikos, K., & Smith, C. (1992). *Signing naturally level 2: Student workbook*. DawnSign Press.

Lentz, E. M., Mikos, K., & Smith, C. (2014). *Signing naturally units 7–12: Student workbook*. DawnSign Press.

Lieberman, A. M., Mitchiner, J., & Pontecorvo, E. (2022). Hearing parents learning American Sign Language with their deaf children: A mixed-methods survey. *Applied Linguistics Review*, 1–25. https://doi.org/10.1515/applirev-2021-0120.

Lillo-Martin, D., Gale, E., & Chen Pichler, D. (2021). Family ASL: An early start to equitable education for deaf children. *Topics in Early Childhood Special Education*, 027112142110313. https://doi.org/10.1177/02711214211031307.

Lillo-Martin, D., Goodwin, C., & Prunier, L. (2017, November). *ASL-IPSyn: A new measure of grammatical development (Poster presentation)*. Boston University Conference on Language Development (BUCLD), Boston, MA.

Lillo-Martin, D., & Henner, J. (2021). Acquisition of sign languages. *Annual Review of Linguistics*, *7*(1), 395–419. https://doi.org/10.1146/annurev-linguistics-043020-092357.

Lindert, R. B. (2001). *Hearing families with deaf children: Linguistic and communicative aspects of American Sign Language development* [Doctoral dissertation]. University of California, Berkeley. www.proquest.com/openview/813ca82a49cb50d54d02a8b7a7a9aab2/1?pq-origsite=gscholar&cbl=18750&diss=y.

Looney, D., & Lusin, N. (2019). *Enrollments in languages other than English in United States institutions of higher education, summer 2016 and fall 2016: Final report*. Modern Language Association of America.

Loots, G., & Devisé, I. (2003). The use of visual-tactile communication strategies by deaf and hearing fathers and mothers of deaf infants. *Deaf Studies and Deaf Education*, *8*(1), 31–42.

Lund, E. (2016). Vocabulary knowledge of children with cochlear implants: A meta-analysis. *Journal of Deaf Studies and Deaf Education*, *21*(2), 107–121. https://doi.org/10.1044/2018_AJSLP-16-0239.

Lund, E. (2018). The effects of parent training on vocabulary scores of young children with hearing loss. *American Journal of Speech-Language Pathology*, *27*(2), 765–777. https://doi.org/10.1044/2018_AJSLP-16-0239.

Lytle, L., R., & Oliva, G., A. (2016, April). Raising the whole child: Addressing social-emotional development in deaf children. *Visual Language & Visual*

Learning (VL2) Learning from Science: Research Brief, Research Brief #11. https://vl2.gallaudet.edu/research-briefs/265.

Maluleke, N. P., Khoza-Shangase, K., & Kanji, A. (2021). An integrative review of current practice models and/or process of family-centered early intervention for children who are deaf or hard of hearing. *Family & Community Health: The Journal of Health Promotion & Maintenance, 44* (1), 59–71. https://doi.org/10.1097/FCH.0000000000000276.

Manley, J., Odendahl, J., & Samson, M. (2019). *Early listening at home: Curriculum for infants and toddlers with hearing loss.* Central Institute for the Deaf. https://professionals.cid.edu/product/cid-early-listening-at-home-curriculum/.

Masataka, N. (1996). Perception of motherese in a signed language by 6-month-old deaf infants. *Developmental Psychology, 32*(5), 874–879. http://dx.doi.org.rmuohp.proxy.liblynxgateway.com/10.1037/0012-1649.32 .5.874.

Masataka, N. (1998). Perception of motherese in Japanese Sign Language by 6-month-old hearing infants. *Developmental Psychology, 34*(2), 241–246. http://dx.doi.org.rmuohp.proxy.liblynxgateway.com/10.1037/0012-1649.34 .2.241.

Mathews, E. S. (2011). *Mainstreaming of deaf education in the Republic of Ireland: Language, power, resistance.* [Ph.D. dissertation]. National University of Ireland, Maynooth.

Matthijs, L., Hardonk, S., Sermijn, J. et al. (2017). Mothers of deaf children in the 21st century: Dynamic positioning between the medical and cultural–linguistic discourses. *The Journal of Deaf Studies and Deaf Education, 22*(4), 365–377. https://doi.org/10.1093/deafed/enx021.

McAlexander, S., Picou, E. M., Day, B., Jirik, K. J., Morrison, A. K., & Tharpe, A. M. (2022). *An evaluation of newborn hearing screening brochures and parental understanding of screening result terminology.* EHDI, Virtual Conference, March 13–15, 2022. https://ehdiconference.org/archive/2022/ index.cfm.

McElrath, E., & McDowell, K. (2008). Pedagogical strategies for building community in graduate level distance education courses. *MERLOT Journal of Online Learning and Teaching, 4*(1), 117–127. https://jolt.merlot.org/ vol4no1/mcelrath0308.pdf.

McWilliam, R. A. (2010a). Assessing families' needs with the Routines-Based Interview. In R. A. McWilliam (Ed.), *Working with families of young children with special needs* (pp. 27–59). Guilford Press.

McWilliam, R. A. (2010b). Introduction. In R. A. McWilliam (Ed.), *Working with families of young children with special needs* (pp. 1–7). Guilford Press.

McWilliam, R. A. (2016). The routines-based model for supporting speech and language. *Revista de logopedia, foniatría y audiología*, *36*(4), 178–184. https://doi.org/10.1016/j.rlfa.2016.07.005.

Meier, R. P. (2016). *Sign language acquisition*. Oxford University Press.

Mikos, K., Smith, C., & Lentz, E. M. (2001). *Signing naturally level 3: Student workbook*. DawnSign Press.

Mitchell, R. E., & Karchmer, M. (2004). Chasing the mythical ten percent: Parental hearing status of deaf and hard of hearing students in the United States. *Sign Language Studies*, *4*(2), 138–163.

Mitchiner, J., Nussbaum, D., B., & Scott, S. (2012, June). The implications of bimodal bilingual approaches for children with cochlear implants. *Visual Language & Visual Learning (VL2) Learning from Science: Research Brief, Research Brief #6*. https://vl2.gallaudet.edu/research-briefs/260.

Moeller, M. P. (2000). Early intervention and language development in children who are deaf and hard of hearing. *Pediatrics*, *106*(3), e43. https://doi.org/10.1542/peds.106.3.e43.

Moeller, M. P., Carr, G., Seaver, L., Stredler-Brown, A., & Holzinger, D. (2013). Best practices in family-centered early intervention for children who are deaf or hard of hearing: An international consensus statement. *Journal of Deaf Studies and Deaf Education*, *18*(4), 429–445. https://doi.org/10.1093/deafed/ent034.

Moeller, M. P., White, K. R., & Shisler, L. (2006). Primary care physicians' knowledge, attitudes, and practices related to newborn hearing screening. *Pediatrics*, *118*(4), 1357–1370. https://doi.org/10.1542/peds.2006-1008.

Moonbug Entertainment. (2022). MyGo! Sign language for kids – ASL. www.youtube.com/channel/UCygtj8VfAI0Sez4S7u65kPg.

Morford, J. P., Shaffer, B., Shin, N., Twitchell, P., & Petersen, B. T. (2019). An exploratory study of ASL demonstratives. *Languages*, *4*(4), 80. http://dx.doi.org/10.3390/languages4040080.

Morgan, G., Curtin, M., & Botting, N. (2021). The interplay between early social interaction, language and executive function development in deaf and hearing infants. *Infant Behavior and Development*, *64*, 101591. https://doi.org/10.1016/j.infbeh.2021.101591.

Mostafavi, F., Mahdi Hazavehei, S. M., Oryadi-Zanjani, M. M., Sharifi Rad, G., Rezaianzadeh, A., & Ravanyar, L. (2017). Phenomenological needs assessment of parents of children with cochlear implants. *Electronic Physician*, *9*(9), 5339–5348. https://doi.org/10.19082/5339.

NADvlogs (Director). (2018a, February 28). Gift of love [Video]. https://youtu.be/bRNTiv97lgg.

NADvlogs (Director). (2018b, March 9). Gift of independence [Video]. https://youtu.be/vbVsAHkUfLc.

Napier, J., Leigh, G., & Nann, S. (2007). Teaching sign language to hearing parents of deaf children: An action research process. *Deafness and Education International, 9*(2), 83–100. https://doi.org/10.1002/dei.214.

National Association of the Deaf. (2022a). Early intervention services. www.nad.org/resources/early-intervention-for-infants-and-toddlers/information-for-parents/early-intervention-services/.

National Association of the Deaf. (2022b). Family. www.nad.org/gift-of-language/gift-of-language-family/.

Neumann, K., Chadha, S., Tavartkiladze, G., Bu, X., & White, K. (2019). Newborn and infant hearing screening facing globally growing numbers of people suffering from disabling hearing loss. *International Journal of Neonatal Screening, 5*(1), 7. https://doi.org/10.3390/ijns5010007.

Newport, E. L. (1991). Contrasting concepts of the critical period for language. In S. Carey & R. Gelman (Eds.), *The epigenesis of mind: Essays on biology and cognition* (pp. 111–130). Erlbaum.

Nicastri, M., Giallini, I., Ruoppolo, G. et al. (2021). Parent training and communication empowerment of children with cochlear implant. *Journal of Early Intervention, 43*(2), 117–134. https://doi.org/10.1177/105381512 0922908.

Nickbakht, M., Meyer, C., Scarinci, N., & Beswick, R. (2019). A qualitative investigation of families' needs in the transition to early intervention after diagnosis of hearing loss. *Child: Care, Health & Development, 45*(5), 670–680. https://doi.org/10.1111/cch.12697.

Niparko, J. K., Tobey, E. A., Thal, D. J. et al. (2010). Spoken language development in children following cochlear implantation. *Journal of the American Medical Association, 303*(15), 1498–1506.

Nittrouer, S., Lowenstein, J. H., & Antonelli, J. (2019). Parental language input to children with hearing loss: Does it matter in the end? *Journal of Speech, Language, and Hearing Research, 63*(1), 234–258. https://doi.org/10.1044/2019_JSLHR-19-00123.

O'Brien, C. (2021, July 21). Hearing families learning Irish Sign Language to communicate with their deaf child: A Ph.D. study using grounded theory methodology.Child and Youth Research Summer Seminar Series, Dublin, Ireland. [Virtual Conference presentation].

O'Toole, C., Lyons, R., & Houghton, C. (2021). A qualitative evidence synthesis of parental experiences and perceptions of parent–child interaction therapy for preschool children with communication difficulties. *Journal of*

Speech, Language, and Hearing Research, *64*(8), 3159–3185. https://doi .org/10.1044/2021_JSLHR-20-00732.

Octaberlina, L. R., & Muslimin, A. I. (2020). EFL students perspective towards online learning barriers and alternatives using Moodle/Google Classroom during COVID-19 pandemic. *International Journal of Higher Education, 9* (6), 1–9. https://doi.org/10.5430/ijhe.v9n6p1.

Office of Research Support and International Affairs (RSIA). (2014). *Regional and national summary report of data from the 2013–14 annual survey of deaf and hard of hearing children and youth*. Gallaudet University. www.gallau det.edu/documents/Research-Support-and-International-Affairs/Intl% 20Affairs/Demographics/AS14_RegNat.pdf.

Ortega, G., & Morgan, G. (2015). Phonological development in hearing learn- ers of a sign language: The influence of phonological parameters, sign complexity, and iconicity. *Language Learning, 65*(3), 660–688. https://doi .org/10.1111/lang.12123.

Oyserman, J., & De Geus, M. (2021a). Implementing a new design in parent sign language teaching: The Common European Framework of Reference for Languages. In K. Snoddon & J. C. Weber (Eds.), *Critical perspectives on plurilingualism in deaf education* (pp. 173–194). Multilingual Matters.

Oyserman, J., & De Geus, M. (2021b). *We sign: Parent modules*. EDU-SIGN. www.edu-sign.com/.

Padden, C. A. (1996). Early bilingual lives of deaf children. In I. Parasnis (Ed.), *Cultural and language diversity and the deaf experience* (1st ed., pp. 99–116). Cambridge University Press. www.cambridge.org/core/books/abs/ cultural-and-language-diversity-and-the-deaf-experience/early-bilingual- lives-of-deaf-children/2A96543F783D59A56795F3773B171610.

Pannell, J., Partsch, F., & Fuller, N. (2017). The output hypothesis: From theory to practice. *TESOL Working Paper Series, 15*, 126–159.

Papoušek, M., Papoušek, H., & Haekel, M. (1987). Didactic adjustments in fathers' and mothers' speech to their 3-month-old infants. *Journal of Psycholinguistic Research, 16*(5), 491–516. https://doi.org/10.1007/ BF01073274.

Pénicaud, S., Klein, D., Zatorre, R. J. et al. (2013). Structural brain changes linked to delayed first language acquisition in congenitally deaf individuals. *NeuroImage, 66*, 42–49. https://doi.org/10.1016/j.neuroimage.2012.09.076.

Pittman, P., Benedict, B. S., Olson, S., & Sass-Lehrer, M. (2016). Collaboration with deaf and hard-of-hearing communities. In M. Sass- Lehrer (Ed.), *Early intervention for deaf and hard-of-hearing infants, toddlers, and their families: Interdisciplinary perspectives* (pp. 135–166). Oxford University Press.

Pizer, G., Meier, R. P., & Points, K. S. (2011). Child-directed signing as a linguistic register. In R. Channon & H. van der Hulst (Eds.), *Formational units in sign languages* (pp. 65–86). de Gruyter. https://doi.org/10.1515/9781614510680.65.

Pudans-Smith, K. K., Cue, K. R., Wolsey, J.-L. A., & Clark, M. D. (2019). To Deaf or not to deaf: That is the question. *Psychology, 10*(15), 2091–2114. https://doi.org/10.4236/psych.2019.1015135.

Purple Moontower. (2022). *TRUE+WAY ASL teacher and student etextbook* (3rd ed.). Purple Moontower. https://truewayasl.com/.

Puyaltó, C., Gaucher, C., & Beaton, A. (2018). Is the right to access to the services and supports ensured for the deaf and hard-of-hearing children? An ethnographic study based on the experience of hearing parents. *Societies, 8* (3), 53. https://doi.org/10.3390/soc8030053.

Quiñonez Summer, L. (2022). Language acquisition for the bilingual child: A perspective on raising bilingual children in the U.S. In L. R. Schmeltz (Ed.), *The NCHAM eBook: A resource guide for Early Hearing Detection and Intervention (EHDI)* (pp. 1–12). National Center for Hearing Assessment and Management, Utah State University.

Rajesh, V., & Venkatesh, L. (2019). Preliminary evaluation of a low-intensity parent training program on speech-language stimulation for children with language delay. *International Journal of Pediatric Otorhinolaryngology, 122*, 99–104. https://doi.org/10.1016/j.ijporl.2019.03.034.

Rems-Smario, Julie (Director). (2017a, February 26). Meet the Kadu family! [Video]. https://youtu.be/o2cqj7Imu1k.

Rems-Smario, Julie (Director). (2017b, November 1). Meet Norah and her family – LEAD-K Campaign for Deaf Kids [Video]. https://youtu.be/exM5EZNY6Ao.

Roberts, M. Y. (2018). Parent-implemented communication treatment for infants and toddlers with hearing loss: A randomized pilot trial. *Journal of Speech, Language, and Hearing Research, 62*(1), 143–152. https://doi.org/10.1044/2018_JSLHR-L-18-0079.

Roberts, M. Y., Hensle, T., & Brooks, M. K. (2016). More than 'try this at home': Including parents in early intervention. *Perspectives of the ASHA Special Interest Groups, 1*(1), 130–143. https://doi.org/10.1044/persp1.SIG1.130

Roberts, M. Y., & Kaiser, A. P. (2011). The effectiveness of parent-implemented language interventions: A meta-analysis. *American Journal of Speech-Language Pathology, 20*(3), 180–199. https://doi.org/10.1044/1058-0360 (2011/10-0055).

Roberts, M. Y., Kaiser, A. P., Wolfe, C. E., Bryant, J. D., & Spidalieri, A. M. (2014). Effects of the Teach-Model-Coach-Review instructional approach on caregiver use of language support strategies and children's expressive language skills. *Journal of Speech, Language, and Hearing Research, 57*(5), 1851–1869. https://doi.org/10.1044/2014_JSLHR-L-13-0113.

Rocky Mountain Deaf School. (2022). RMDSCO. www.youtube.com/user/RMDSCO/featured.

Rosen, R. S. (2010). American Sign Language curricula: A review. *Sign Language Studies, 10*, 348–381. https://doi.org/10.1353/sls.0.0050.

Saint-Georges, C., Chetouani, M., Cassel, R. et al. (2013). Motherese in interaction: At the cross-road of emotion and cognition? (A systematic review). *PLOS ONE, 8*(10): e78103. https://doi.org/10.1371/journal.pone.0078103.

Santos, S., & Cordes, S. (2022). Math abilities in deaf and hard of hearing children: The role of language in developing number concepts. *Psychological Review, 129*(1), 199–211. https://doi.org/10.1037/rev0000303.

Sass-Lehrer, M., Porter, A., & Wu, C. L. (2016). Families: Partnerships in practice. In M. Sass-Lehrer (Ed.), *Early intervention for deaf and hard-of-hearing infants, toddlers, and their families: Interdisciplinary perspectives* (pp. 65–103). Oxford University Press.

Shearer, A. E., Shen, J., Amr, S., Morton, C. C., & Smith, R. J. (2019). A proposal for comprehensive newborn hearing screening to improve identification of deaf and hard-of-hearing children. *Genetics in Medicine, 21*(11), 2614–2630. https://doi.org/10.1038/s41436-019-0563-5.

Shezi, Z. M., & Joseph, L. N. (2021). Parental views on informational counselling provided by audiologists for children with permanent childhood hearing loss. *South African Journal of Communication Disorders, 68*(1). https://doi.org/10.4102/sajcd.v68i1.799.

SignOn. (2022). SignOn Connect – Immerse yourself in the deaf ASL community. https://signonconnect.com/.

Simms, L., Kite, B. J., Scott, S., & Burns, H. (Directors). (2016, May 24). Maximizing language acquisition: ASL and spoken English [Video]. https://youtu.be/2e4EMWM29JI.

Singleton, J. L., & Newport, E. L. (2004). When learners surpass their models: The acquisition of American Sign Language from inconsistent input. *Cognitive Psychology, 49*(4), 370–407. https://doi.org/10.1016/j.cogpsych.2004.05.001.

SKI-HI Institute. (2001). Deaf mentor curriculum: A resource manual for home-based, bilingual-bicultural programming for young children who are deaf or hard of hearing and their families. HOPE Inc. https://hopepubl.com/product/ski-hi-curriculum/.

Skotara, N., Salden, U., Kügow, M., Hänel-Faulhaber, B., & Röder, B. (2012). The influence of language deprivation in early childhood on L2 processing: An ERP comparison of deaf native signers and deaf signers with a delayed language acquisition. *BMC Neuroscience, 13*(44), 1–14. https://doi.org/10.1186/1471-2202-13-44.

Smith, C., Lentz, E. M., & Mikos, K. (2008a). *Signing naturally units 1–6: Student workbook.* DawnSign Press. www.dawnsign.com/products/details/signing-naturally-units-1-6-student-set.

Smith, C., Lentz, E. M., & Mikos, K. (2008b). *Signing naturally units 1–6: Teacher's curriculum guide.* DawnSign Press. www.dawnsign.com/products/details/signing-naturally-units-1-6-student-set.

Snoddon, K. (2015). Using the Common European Framework of Reference for Languages to teach sign language to parents of deaf children. *Canadian Modern Language Review, 71*(3), 270–287. https://doi.org/10.3138/cmlr.2602.

Spencer, P. E. (2001). *A good start: Suggestions for visual conversations with deaf and hard of hearing babies and toddlers.* Gallaudet University Laurent Clerc National Deaf Education Center.

Stika, C. J., Eisenberg, L. S., Johnson, K. C. et al. (2015). Developmental outcomes of early-identified children who are hard of hearing at 12 to 18 months of age. *Early Human Development, 91*(1), 47–55. https://doi.org/10.1016/j.earlhumdev.2014.11.005.

Su, P. L., & Roberts, M. Y. (2019). Quantity and quality of parental utterances and responses to children with hearing loss prior to cochlear implant. *Journal of Early Intervention, 41*(4), 366–387. https://doi.org/10.1177/1053815119867286.

Sultana, N., Wong, L. L. N., & Purdy, S. C. (2019). Analysis of amount and style of oral interaction related to language outcomes in children with hearing loss: A systematic review (2006–2016). *Journal of Speech, Language, and Hearing Research, 62*(9), 3470–3492. https://doi.org/10.1044/2019_JSLHR-L-19-0076.

Swain, M. (2005). The output hypothesis: Theory and research. In E. Hinkel (Ed.), *Handbook on research in second language learning and teaching* (pp. 471–483). Lawrence Erlbaum.

Szagun, G., & Schramm, S. A. (2016). Sources of variability in language development of children with cochlear implants: Age at implantation, parental language, and early features of children's language construction. *Journal of Child Language, 43*(3), 505–536. https://doi.org/10.1017/S0305000915000641.

The Hanen Centre. (2019). About the Hanen Centre: Helping you help children communicate. www.hanen.org/About-Us.aspx.

Thomson, V., & Yoshinaga-Itano, C. (2018). The role of audiologists in assuring follow-up to outpatient screening in early hearing detection and intervention systems. *American Journal of Audiology, 27*(3), 283–293. https://doi.org/10.1044/2018_AJA-17-0113.

Tomasello, M., & Farrar, M. J. (1986). Joint attention and early language. *Child Development, 57*(6), 1454–1463. https://doi.org/10.2307/1130423.

Trivette, C. M., Dunst, C. J., Hamby, D. W., & O'Herin, C. E. (2009). Characteristics and consequences of adult learning methods and strategies. *Tots n Tech Research Institute, 3*(1), 1–33.

Twitchell, P., Shin, N., Shaffer, B., Wilkinson, E., & Morford, J. P. (2022). Demonstratives in ASL. *Theoretical Issues in Sign Language Research.* www.dropbox.com/s/fky2buyfm0oyyim/TISLR14_Abstract_S-05_216.pdf?dl=0.

Ullman, M. T. (2015). The declarative/procedural model: A neurobiologically motivated theory of first and second language. In B. VanPatten & J. Williams (Eds.) *Theories in second language acquisition: An introduction* (2nd ed., pp. 135–158). Routledge.

University of the Free State. (2022). South African Sign Language short learning programmes. Department of South African Sign Language and Deaf Studies (Incorporating ULFE). www.ufs.ac.za/sasl/department-of-south-african-sign-language-and-deaf-studies-(incorporating-the-unit-for-language-facilitation-and-empowerment)/academic-activities/sasl-short-learning-programme.

VanPatten, B. (2015). Input processing in adult SLA. In B. VanPatten & J. Williams (Eds.), *Theories in second language acquisition: An introduction* (2nd ed., pp. 113–134). Routledge.

Ventayen, R. J. M., Estira, K. L. A., Guzman, M. J. D., Cabaluna, C. M., & Espinosa, N. N. (2018). Usability evaluation of Google Classroom: Basis for the adaptation of GSuite e-learning platform. *Asia Pacific Journal of Education, 5*(1), 47–51.

Vishwakarma, A., & Kulshrestha, P. (2022, June 24). Impact of Covid19 pandemic on early sign language acquisition [Conference presentation]. 4th International Conference on Sign Language Acquisition (ICSLA), Boston, June 23–25, 2022. Virtual conference. https://whova.com/portal/webapp/icsla1_202206/Agenda/2384873.

Vonen, A. M. (2019, June 14). *Se mitt språk – See my language.* Oslo Metropolitan University.

Watkins, S., Pittman, P., & Walden, B. (1998). The deaf mentor experimental project for young children who are deaf and their families. *American Annals of the Deaf, 143*(1), 29–34. https://doi.org/10.1353/aad.2012.0098.

Weitzman, E. (2017). *It takes two to talk: A practical guide for parents of children with language delays* (5th ed.). Hanen Centre. www.hanen.org/Guidebooks/Parents/It-Takes-Two-to-Talk.aspx.

Wilkinson, E., Lepic, R., & Hou, L. (2023). Usage-based grammar: Multi-word expressions in American Sign Language. In T. Janzen & B. Shaffer (Eds.), *Signed language and gesture research in cognitive linguistics*. De Gruyter Mouton.

Wright, B., Hargate, R., Garside, M. et al. (2021). A systematic scoping review of early interventions for parents of deaf infants. *BMC Pediatrics*, *21*(1), 467. https://doi.org/10.1186/s12887-021-02893-9.

Wroblewska-Seniuk, K. E., Dabrowski, P., Szyfter, W., & Mazela, J. (2017). Universal newborn hearing screening: Methods and results, obstacles, and benefits. *Pediatric Research*, *81*(3), 415–422. https://doi.org/10.1038/pr.2016.250.

Yorkston, K., Dowden, P., Honsinger, M., Marriner, N., & Smith, K. (1988). A comparison of standard and user vocabulary lists. *Augmentative and Alternative Communication*, *4*(4), 189–210. https://doi.org/10.1080/07434618812331274807.

Yoshinaga-Itano, C., Sedey, A. L., Wiggin, M., & Chung, W. (2017). Early hearing detection and vocabulary of children with hearing loss. *Pediatrics*, *140*(2), e20162964. https://doi.org/10.1542/peds.2016-2964.

Yosso, T. J. (2005). Whose culture has capital? A critical race theory discussion of community cultural wealth. *Race Ethnicity and Education*, *8*(1), 69–91. https://doi.org/10.1080/1361332052000341006.

Zaidman-Zait, A. (2008). Everyday problems and stress faced by parents of children with cochlear implants. *Rehabilitation Psychology*, *53*(2), 139–152. https://doi.org/10.1037/0090-5550.53.2.139.

Zarchy, R. M., & Geer, L. C. (2020). *American Sign Language at home: A family curriculum*. Book Baby.

Zarchy, R. M., & Geer, L. C. (2022, June 25). Teaching hearing parents ASL to enrich language at home. International Conference on Sign Language Acquisition (ICSLA), Boston, June 23–25, 2022. Virtual conference. https://sites.bu.edu/icsla/conference-information/schedule-and-abstracts/

Zarchy, R. M., & Geer, L. C. (2023). *American Sign Language at home: A family curriculum* (2nd ed.). Solificatio.

Acknowledgments

We are grateful to Drs. David Quinto-Pozos and Erin Wilkinson for inviting us to contribute this Element to the series on signed languages. We appreciate the support and feedback they have provided in developing this manuscript as well as the two anonymous reviewers who provided helpful comments on section restructuring and ideas for tightening up the manuscript. We would also like to thank everyone who has used *ASL at Home* and shared feedback on the curriculum from a user perspective. Thank you also to attendees and fellow presenters at ICSLA 4 for engaging with us on this topic. Your insights helped to shape this Element.

Cambridge Elements ⁼

Sign Languages

Erin Wilkinson

University of New Mexico

Erin Wilkinson is Associate Professor in the Department of Linguistics at the University of New Mexico. She has broad research interests in bilingualism and multilingualism, language documentation and description, language change and variation, signed language typology, and language planning and policy in highly diverse signing communities. Her current studies in collaboration with other researchers examine cognitive and linguistic processing in signing bilingual populations. She also explores what linguistic structures are re-structured over time in signed languages and what are possible factors that contribute to language change and variation in signed languages in the lens of usage-based theory.

David Quinto-Pozos

University of Texas at Austin

David Quinto-Pozos is an Associate Professor in the Department of Linguistics at the University of Texas at Austin. His research interests include signed language contact and change, the interaction of language and gesture, L1 and L2 signed language acquisition, spoken-signed language interpretation, and vocabulary knowledge and literacy. He has served as an editor/co-editor of four volumes on signed language research, including *Modality and Structure in Signed and Spoken Languages* (Meier, Cormier, & Quinto-Pozos, eds. 2002; Cambridge University Press), *Sign Languages in Contact* (Quinto-Pozos, ed. 2007; Gallaudet University Press), *Multilingual Aspects of Signed Language Communication and Disorder* (Quinto-Pozos, 2014; Multilingual Matters), and *Toward Effective Practice: Interpreting in Spanish-influenced Settings* (Annarino, Aponte-Samalot, & Quinto-Pozos, 2014; National Consortium of Interpreter Education Centers).

About the Series

This Elements series covers a broad range of topics on signed language structure and use, describing dozens of different signed languages, along with accounts of signing (deaf and non-deaf) communities. The series is accessible (via print, electronic media, and video-based summaries) to a large deaf/signing-friendly audience

Cambridge Elements ☰

Sign Languages

Elements in the series

A Family-Centered Signed Language Curriculum to Support Deaf Children's Language Acquisition
Razi M. Zarchy and Leah C. Geer

A full series listing is available at: www.cambridge.org/EISL

Printed in the United States
by Baker & Taylor Publisher Services